CORE CONCEPTS IN CULTURAL ANTHROPOLOGY

SECOND EDITION

Robert H. Lavenda

Emily A. Schultz

St. Cloud State University

Mc
Graw
Hill

Boston   Burr Ridge, IL   Dubuque, IA   Madison, WI   New York
San Francisco   St. Louis   Bangkok   Bogotá   Caracas   Kuala Lumpur
Lisbon   London   Madrid   Mexico City   Milan   Montreal   New Delhi
Santiago   Seoul   Singapore   Sydney   Taipei   Toronto

McGraw-Hill Higher Education

A Division of The **McGraw-Hill** *Companies*

1 2 3 4 5 6 7 8 9 0 DOC/DOC 0 9 8 7 6 5 4 3 2

Library of Congress Cataloging-in-Publication Data

Lavenda, Robert H.
   Core concepts in cultural anthropology / Robert H. Lavenda, Emily A.
Schultz. —2nd ed.
      p. cm.
   Includes bibliographical references and index.
   ISBN 0-07-281860-3
      1. Ethnology.   2. Ethnology—Bibliography.   I. Schultz, Emily A. (Emily
Ann), 1949–   II. Title.
GN316.L39 2002
306—dc21

                                           2002069218

Publisher, Phillip A. Butcher; sponsoring editor, Kevin M. Witt; production
editor, Jennifer Chambliss; manuscript editor, Joseph A. Webb; design manager,
Sharon Spurlock; art manager, Emma Ghiselli; text and cover designer, Sharon
Spurlock; photo researcher, Alexandra Ambrose; production supervisor, Pam
Augspurger. The text was set in 11/14 Sabon by TBH Typecast, Inc., and
printed on acid-free 45# New Era Matte by R. R. Donnelley.
Cover image: copyright © Luca Zampedri/nonstock

www.mhhe.com

To Jan Beatty

Contents

◈ Preface ◈

THIS BOOK IS A CONCISE introduction to the fundamental key terms and issues of contemporary cultural anthropology. It is not a condensed version of the fifth edition of our textbook *Cultural Anthropology: A Perspective on the Human Condition;* this is something new. Our goal is to provide students with a rapid sketch of the basic ideas and practices of cultural anthropology in a style analogous to a bibliographic essay. A good bibliographic essay prepares its readers to do their own research by giving them an idea of what sources are available and where and how those sources fit into research in that field. So, too, we hope, with this volume: we want students to know what the core concepts and key terms are in cultural anthropology, how they are related to one another, and where they come from so the students have a context for understanding anthropological writing, especially ethnographic writing, when they turn to it.

Our expectation is that this text will be used in conjunction with ethnographies and/or collections of readings during the term. For that reason, we have omitted ethnographic examples and other kinds of details found in our textbook *Cultural Anthropology* (and in most introductory texts), and we have concentrated on providing a scaffolding on which students can rely as they begin to read anthropological writing.

Features

- *Flexibility.* This text can be used in many different ways. It can be used by itself as a concise introduction to cultural anthropology when the course time that can be devoted to covering the discipline is limited. It can also be used very successfully in conjunction with other readings, either anthologies or ethnographies, or both. *Core Concepts in Cultural Anthropology* may be assigned at the beginning of the term to go along with introductory lectures and be referred to as needed. Another approach, popular with users of the first edition of *Core Concepts in Cultural Anthropology,* is to assign specific chapters to be read along with particular ethnographies or course topics. The book can also be used in upper-level classes where a review of the basic key terms and issues in the field may be valuable, or as a quick way to orient nonanthropology students taking upper-level anthropology courses. To accommodate various uses, we have made each chapter as self-contained as possible and, in the second edition, have added numbered section headings, for ease in assigning specific sections if needed. We have included cross-references to related topics in other chapters wherever possible.

- *Brief and affordable.* What you have in your hands is a framework, a basic orientation to cultural anthropology. One consequence of writing a concise introduction is that many of the details and nuances of the field are left out. We assume that instructors will provide favorite ethnographic examples both in class and in other readings to illustrate the issues they raise in class. It is our hope that the brevity and affordability of this text will allow the assignment of additional course readings and will engender lectures and class discussions that bring back the nuance and subtlety that are a part of every human endeavor, including anthropology, teaching, and learning.

◆ *Provides abundant study aids.* Each chapter opens with a list of key terms discussed in that chapter. Each chapter ends with a concluding paragraph, which summarizes the concepts introduced in the chapter, and a list of suggested readings, which—along with an extensive end-of-book bibliography—directs students to more detailed discussions. An online Study Guide provides additional learning help.

◆ *Includes a chapter on theory.* Because all anthropological writing is theoretically situated, we have included a chapter on theory in cultural anthropology. We think it is important for students to get a sense of where what they are reading fits into a larger historical and theoretical context in anthropology. We also think they need some tools for interpreting what they are reading because ethnographic writing often presents and debates alternative theoretical positions and it is useful for students to know the issues addressed in those positions and raised in the debate.

◆ *Offers a list of ethnographies in print.* A Web site that accompanies the text lists and plots on a world map all available ethnographies in print and provides pertinent information. A list of ethnographies, organized geographically, appears in the front of the instructor's copies as well.

A word about the chapters and where to find certain materials: as we put the book together, we found that some important topics fit better within broader categories. For example, discussion of research methods in anthropology will be found in Chapter 1, "Anthropology," and discussion of gender, race, class, ethnicity, and nonkin forms of social organization is found in Chapter 6, "The Dimensions of Social Organization."

What's New in the Second Edition?

◆ Section headings have been added to make it easier for students to navigate the text and to give instructors additional flexibility should they wish to assign segments of chapters as needed for their particular course organization.

- Discussions of various concepts and terms have been rewritten, revised, or expanded for purposes of clarification.

- The discussion of the culture concept has been expanded and updated.

- Discussions of subsistence patterns, modes of resource distribution, and social organization have been expanded in a way that avoids simple, unidirectional interpretations of cultural evolution. The second edition has a new discussion of Leslie White's approach to cultural evolution and of Marcel Mauss and gift exchange versus commodity exchange. It has new material on globalization and local consumption practices.

- This edition has an expanded discussion of ritual.

- The final part of the theory chapter has been revised to take account of recent developments beyond the positivist/postmodernist debate.

- New material will be found on media and popular culture, with additional material on cyberculture.

- The second edition has new material on hypergamy and on new reproductive technologies.

- Readers will find references to the precapitalist world system centered in India and to contemporary examples of nonwestern capitalism.

- The discussion of caste and class has been updated.

- Cross-reference terminology has been changed to make clear that the cross-reference refers to additional mentions of the term. These may be the original definition, expanded discussions, or additional references to the term.

- Readers will see some additional suggestions for further reading.

Acknowledgments

We'd like to thank the reviewers of this text for their careful comments: Shelly Braun, University of Utah; Martha Kaplan, Vassar College; and Jon McGee, Southwest Texas State University.

Finally, we would like to thank Jan Beatty, who suggested a book like this to us in the first place. It has been an interesting and valuable project for us, as it directed our attention to the various ways in which cultural anthropology might be presented. We hope that you find it to be an effective tool for teaching anthropology to new generations of students.

1

Anthropology

The key terms and concepts covered in this chapter, in the order in which they appear:

anthropology
holistic
comparative
evolutionary

biological anthropology
primatologists
paleoanthropologists
forensic anthropologists

cultural anthropology
culture

fieldwork
informants
participant-observation
monograph

ethnography
ethnology

anthropological linguistics
linguistic anthropology
language
archaeology
prehistory

applied anthropology
development anthropology
objective knowledge

positivism
modernism
postmodernism
reflexive

ANTHROPOLOGY IS A DISCIPLINE that exists at the borders of the social sciences, the humanities, and the biological sciences. The term comes from two Greek words: *anthropos,* meaning "human beings," and *logia,* "the study of." The "study of human beings" would seem to be a rather broad topic for any one field, but anthropologists take the name of their discipline seriously, and anything that has to do with human beings probably is of potential interest to anthropologists. Indeed, **anthropology** can be formally defined as the study of human nature, human society, and the human past. This means that some anthropologists study human origins, others try to understand diverse contemporary ways of life, and some excavate the past or try to understand why we speak the ways we do.

1.1 An Anthropological Perspective

Given its breadth, what coherence anthropology has as a discipline comes from its perspective. Anthropology is holistic, comparative, field based, and evolutionary. For anthropologists, being **holistic** means trying to fit together all that is known about human beings. That is, anthropologists draw on the findings of many different disciplines that study human beings (human biology, economics, and religion, for example), as well as data on similar topics that they have collected, and attempt to produce an encompassing picture of human life. In the same way, when an anthropologist studies a specific group of people, the goal is to produce a holistic portrait of that people's way of life by bringing together information about many different facets of their lives—social, religious, economic, political, linguistic, and so forth—in order to provide a nuanced context for understanding who they are and why they do what they do.

However, to generalize about human nature, human society, and the human past requires information from as wide a range of human groups as possible. Anthropologists realized long ago that the patterns of life common in their own societies were not necessarily followed in other societies. And so, anthropology is a **comparative** discipline: anthropologists must consider similarities and differences in as wide a range of human societies as possible before generalizing about what it means to be human.

Because anthropology is interested in human beings in all places and at all times, anthropologists are curious about how we got to be what we are today. For this reason, anthropology is **evolutionary.** A major branch of anthropology is concerned with the study of the biological evolution of the human species over time, including the study of human origins and genetic variety and inheritance in living human populations. Some anthropologists have also been interested in cultural evolution, looking for patterns of orderly change over time in socially acquired behavior that is not carried in the genes.

1.2 The Subfields of Anthropology

Anthropology in North America historically has been divided into four major subfields: biological anthropology, cultural anthropology, linguistic anthropology, and archaeology.

Biological anthropology is the subfield of anthropology that looks at human beings as biological organisms. Biological anthropologists are interested in many different aspects of human biology, including our similarities to and differences from other living organisms. Those who study the closest living relatives of human beings—the nonhuman primates (chimpanzees and gorillas, for example)—are called primatologists. Those who specialize in the study of the fossilized bones and teeth of our earliest ancestors are called paleoanthropologists. Other biological anthropologists examine the genetic variation among and within different human populations or investigate variation in human skeletal biology (for example, measuring and comparing the shapes and sizes of bones or teeth using skeletal remains from different human populations). Newer specialties focus on human adaptability in different ecological settings, on human growth and development, and on the connections between a population's evolutionary history and its susceptibility to disease. **Forensic anthropologists** use their knowledge of human anatomy to aid law-enforcement and human-rights investigators by assisting in the identification of skeletal material found at crime or accident sites or at sites associated with possible human-rights violations.

Cultural anthropology (sometimes called social anthropology in Great Britain) is another major subfield of anthropology. Cultural anthropologists investigate how variation in the beliefs and behaviors of members of different human groups is shaped by **culture,** sets of learned behaviors and ideas that human beings acquire as members of society. (For a fuller discussion of the concept of culture, see Chapter 2.) Cultural anthropologists specialize in specific domains of human cultural activity. Some study the ways people organize themselves to carry out collective tasks, whether economic, political, or spiritual. Others focus on the forms and meanings of expressive behavior in human societies—language, art, music, ritual, religion, and the like. Still others examine material culture—the things people make and use, such as clothing, housing, tools, and the techniques they employ to get food and produce material goods. They may also study the ways in which technologies and environments shape each other. For some time, cultural anthropologists have been interested in the way non-Western peoples have responded to the political and economic challenges of European colonialism and the capitalist industrial technology that came with it. They investigate contemporary issues of gender and sexuality, transnational labor migration, and the post–Cold War resurgence of ethnicity and nationalism around the world. And some cultural anthropologists have started to examine the increasing influence of computer technology on the social and cultural life of peoples throughout the world.

In all of these cases, the comparative nature of anthropology requires that what is taken for granted by members of a specific society—the anthropologist's own, as much as any other—must be examined, or "problematized." As a result, there is a double movement in anthropology: anthropologists study other ways of life not only to understand them in their own terms but also to put the anthropologists' own ways of life in perspective.

To make their discipline comparative, cultural anthropologists began to immerse themselves in the lives of other peoples. Traditionally, cultural anthropology is rooted in **fieldwork,** an anthropologist's personal, long-term experience with a specific group of people and their way of life. Where possible, anthropologists try to live for a year or more with the people whose way of life is of concern to them. The result is a fine-grained knowledge of the everyday details of life. Cultural anthropologists get to know people as individuals, not as "data sets." They remember the names and faces of people who, over the course of a year or more, have become familiar to them as complex and complicated men, women, and children. They remember the feel of the noonday sun, the sounds of the morning, the smells of food cooking, the pace and rhythm of life. In this sense, anthropology traditionally has been an *experiential* discipline. This approach does, of course, have drawbacks as well as advantages: Anthropologists are not usually able to make macrolevel generalizations about an entire nation or society, and their attention is not usually directed toward national or international policy-making or data collection. They are often, however, well aware of the *effects* of national or international decisions on the local level. In fact, in recent years, a number of anthropologists have done illuminating work about nations, refugees and migrations, and international and global processes.

People who share information about their way of life with anthropologists traditionally have been called **informants.** In recent years, however, a number of anthropologists have become uncomfortable with that term, which to some conjures up images of police informers and to others seems to reduce fully rounded individuals to the information they provide. But anthropologists have not been able to agree on an expression that might replace informant; some prefer "respondent" or "teacher" or "friend" or simply refer to "the people with whom I work." Regardless of the term, fieldworkers gain insight into another way of life by taking part as fully as they can in a group's social activities, as well as by observing those activities as outsiders. This research method, known as **participant-observation,** is central to cultural anthropology. Cultural anthropologists also use a variety of other

To achieve information

research methods, including interviews, censuses, surveys, and even statistical sampling techniques when appropriate.

Cultural anthropologists write about what they have learned in scholarly articles or in books, and sometimes they document the lives of their research subjects on film. The word **monograph** is sometimes used to describe the books that anthropologists write; an ethnographic monograph, or **ethnography,** is a scholarly work about a specific way of life. **Ethnology** is the comparative study of two or more ways of life. Thus, cultural anthropologists who write ethnographies are sometimes called *ethnographers,* and anthropologists who compare ethnographic information on many different ways of life are sometimes called *ethnologists.* The prefix "ethno-" comes from the Greek *ethnos* (people) and is used a great deal by anthropologists to mean "of (or about) a people" or "of (or about) an ethnic group."

ethno-graphy → scholarly work about spec, way of life.

A third major subfield of anthropology, called **anthropological linguistics** or **linguistic anthropology,** is the branch of anthropology concerned with the study of human languages. For many people, the most striking cultural feature of human beings is **language,** the system of arbitrary vocal symbols we use to encode our experience of the world and of one another. Anthropological linguists were some of the first people to transcribe non-Western languages and to produce grammars and dictionaries of those languages. They also have worked to show the ways in which a people's language (or languages) serves as the main carrier of important cultural information. In tracing the relationships between language and culture, these anthropologists have investigated a range of topics (see Chapter 3 for details).

language Vocal symbols used to encode our experience

In all their research, anthropological linguists seek to understand language in relation to the broader cultural, historical, or biological contexts that make it possible. Modern anthropological linguists are trained in both formal linguistics and anthropology, and some cultural anthropologists study linguistics as part of their professional preparation.

Archaeology, the fourth traditional subfield of North American anthropology, can be defined as a cultural anthropology of the human past, involving the analysis of the material remains of ear-

Study of remains of human societies.

lier human societies. Through archaeology, anthropologists discover much about human history, particularly **prehistory,** the long stretch of time before the development of writing. Archaeologists look for evidence of past human cultural activity, such as postholes, garbage heaps, and settlement patterns. Depending on the locations and ages of the sites they are digging, archaeologists may also have to be experts in stone-tool manufacture, metallurgy, or ancient pottery. Because archaeological excavations frequently uncover remains such as bones or plant pollen, archaeologists often work in teams with other scientists who specialize in the analysis of those remains.

The work archaeologists do complements the work done by other kinds of anthropologists. For example, paleontologists may find that archaeological information about successive stone-tool traditions in a particular region may correlate with fossil evidence of prehistoric occupation of that region by ancient human populations. Cultural anthropologists may use the work of archaeologists to help them interpret contemporary patterns of land use or forms of subsistence technology.

While popular media often portray archaeologists as concerned primarily with exotic ancient "stuff" (the "Indiana Jones syndrome," we might call it), archaeologists are usually more interested in seeking answers to cultural questions that can only be addressed properly by considering the passage of time. For example, archaeologists can use dating techniques to establish the ages of artifacts, which then allows them to hypothesize about patterns of sociocultural change in ancient societies. That is, tracing the spread of cultural inventions over time from one site to another allows them to hypothesize about the nature and degree of social contact between different peoples. Some contemporary archaeologists even dig through layers of garbage deposited by people within the past two or three decades, often uncovering surprising information about modern consumption patterns. (Table 1.1 lists the four traditional subfields of anthropology.)

In recent decades, increasing numbers of anthropologists have been using the methods and findings from every subfield of anthropology to address problems in the contemporary world, in

TABLE 1.1   The Traditional Subfields of Anthropology

Biological anthropology
Cultural anthropology
Linguistic anthropology
Archaeology

what is called **applied anthropology.** This subfield has grown rapidly as an area of involvement and employment for anthropologists. Some applied anthropologists may use a particular group's ideas about illness and health to introduce new public-health practices in a way that makes sense to and will be accepted by members of that group. Others may apply knowledge of traditional social organization to ease the problems of refugees trying to settle in a new land. Still others may tap their knowledge of traditional and Western methods of cultivation to help farmers increase their crop yields. Taken together, these activities are sometimes called **development anthropology** because their aim is to improve people's capacities to maintain their health, produce their food, and otherwise adapt to the challenges of life in the contemporary world.

Applied anthropologists with a background in archaeology may be involved with contract or salvage archaeology, or they may work in cultural resource management to ensure that the human past is not destroyed by, say, the construction of new buildings, highways, or dams. Biological anthropologists may become involved in forensic work, such as the determination of social characteristics of crime or accident victims, or in nutrition.

In recent years, increasing numbers of anthropologists have come to view applied anthropology as a separate field of professional specialization—related to the other four fields but with its own techniques and theoretical questions. More and more universities in the United States have begun to develop courses and programs in applied anthropology.

While anthropology may have begun in Western Europe and the United States more than a century ago, over the course of its history it has become an international discipline. Universities and research institutions in many countries around the world have established anthropology departments, offer courses and degrees, and carry out research, both theoretical and applied. Anthropologists in different countries have established national anthropological associations, and there are also international associations of anthropologists for the dissemination of anthropological research.

1.3 Is Anthropology a Science: Modernism, Postmodernism, and Beyond

At the beginning of the twentieth century, most anthropologists viewed their growing discipline as a science. They agreed that the truth about the world was accessible through the five senses; that a properly disciplined rational mind could derive universal, objective truths from material evidence; and that a single scientific method could be applied to any dimension of reality, from the movement of the planets to human sexual behavior. Such investigation was supposed to produce **objective knowledge:** undistorted, and thus universally valid, knowledge about the world. Anthropologists felt free to apply scientific methods in any area of anthropological interest, from stone tools to religion, confident that the combined results of these efforts would produce a genuine "Science of Man" (as it was then called). This set of ideas and practices is known as **positivism.**

Today, many critical observers of the natural and social sciences connect these ideas to a complex Western cultural ideology called **modernism.** Modernism can be (and has been) viewed in terms of liberation from outdated traditions that prevent people from building better lives for themselves and their children. Critics have argued, however, that modern Western science, rather than being a universal path to objective truth, is itself a culture-bound enterprise connected to a specific definition of progress. Many members of non-Western societies agree with these critics that in their experience, modernist ideas have been used by powerful

Western states to dominate them and to undermine their traditional beliefs and practices. From their perspective, Western-style "progress" has meant the loss of political autonomy, an increase in economic impoverishment and environmental degradation, and destruction of systems of social relations and values that clash with the "modern" way of life.

Result → [handwritten margin note]

This criticism of modernism, accompanied by an active questioning of all the boundaries and categories that modernists set up as objectively true, has come to be called **postmodernism.** Its plausibility as an intellectual position increased after the end of the Cold War in 1989, when many previously unquestioned cultural and political "truths" about the world seemed to crumble overnight. To be postmodern is to question the universalizing tendencies of modernism, especially of modernist understandings of science. Postmodernists point out that people occupying powerful social positions often are able to pass off their own cultural or political prejudices as universal truths, while dismissing or ignoring alternative views held by powerless groups.

postmodernism of reverting away from modern. [handwritten margin note]

Anthropologists had long considered themselves to be debunkers of distorting Western stereotypes about non-Western peoples. Having frequently defended the integrity of indigenous societies against the onslaughts of modernizing missionaries and "development" experts, they had come to assume that they were on the side of those whose ways of life they studied. From the perspective of some members of those societies, however, as well as from the viewpoint of postmodernists, anthropologists looked just like another group of outside "experts" making their own universal claims about human cultures, behaving no differently from chemists making universal, "expert" claims about molecules.

1.4 Reflexive Anthropology

Postmodern criticism prompted anthropologists to engage in a reappraisal of their discipline and, in particular, to rethink what was involved in fieldwork and the writing of ethnography. While cultural anthropologists continue to value careful observational methods and accurate, systematic data gathering, many of them also take seriously certain parts of the postmodern critique. For example, modeling ethnographers in the field on natural scientists in their laboratories appears problematic once ethnographers grant that the subject matter of anthropology, unlike that of chemistry, consists of human beings, members of the same species as the scientists studying them. Rather than a relationship between a curious human being and inert matter, anthropological fieldwork always involved a social relationship between at least two curious individuals. This meant that the cultural identity and personal characteristics of fieldworkers had to be taken into account when attempting to make sense of their ethnographic writing. Put another way, fieldwork had to become a **reflexive activity**, in which anthropologists carefully scrutinized both their own contribution to fieldwork interactions and the responses these interactions elicited from informants. That is, rather than assuming that they were, for all intents and purposes, invisible to the people they were studying, anthropologists began to consider the effect that they had on the people with whom they were living. They began to recognize that who they were as individuals and as socially-situated actors had an effect on their research. Many contemporary cultural anthropologists have accepted the challenges of doing reflexive fieldwork and are persuaded that such fieldwork produces better, more accurate ethnography than modernist methods ever did. Reflexive fieldworkers are much more explicit about the limitations of their own knowledge and much more generous in the credit they give to their informants. Some have written their ethnographies in new, experimental styles that often read more like novels than scientific texts.

Indeed, many ethnographers today no longer act as outsiders but have taken up the challenge of doing participant-observation in a culture to which they belong. They are conscious of potential pitfalls but are convinced that their professional training will help them provide a unique and valuable perspective. They see their task as finding a way to combine the most valuable elements of the postmodern critique of ethnography with a continuing respect for empirical evidence. The challenge of such a task is great and perhaps as paradoxical as the notion of participant-observation, but many ethnographers believe that this uncomfortable middle ground can yield important insights into human cultural practices, insights that can be secured in no other way.

Indeed, at the beginning of the twenty-first century, many ethnographers (as well as many members of the societies in which they work) have moved beyond the opposition between modernism and postmodernism. They have drawn attention to the ways in which members of non-Western societies selectively incorporate "modern" or "scientific" practices originating in the Western world in order to help them develop their own *alternative modernities*. At the same time, a reconsideration of the nature of "science" by anthropologists and others has shown that the positivist understanding of science may, in fact, offer an incomplete account of scientific successes and failures, not only in the social sciences but also in physical sciences such as physics and biology. This development opens up new and exciting possibilities for alternative understandings of science—and of anthropology as a science—that are yet to be developed.

For Further Reading

BIOLOGICAL ANTHROPOLOGY
Park 1998; Relethford 1996

ARCHAEOLOGY
Ashmore and Sharer 2000

APPLIED ANTHROPOLOGY
Van Willigen 1993

DEVELOPMENT ANTHROPOLOGY
Gardner and Lewis 1996

FIELD RESEARCH
Agar 1996; Behar 1997; Bernard 1994; Bradburd 1998; Rabinow 1977

2

Culture

The key terms and concepts covered in this chapter, in the order in which they appear:

culture
cultural universals
symbols
ethnocentrism
cultural relativism
indigenization

culture

CULTURE HAS LONG BEEN the central concept in anthropology. At its most basic, culture is understood to refer to learned sets of ideas and behaviors that are acquired by people as members of society. Anthropologists have used the concept of culture in a variety of ways over the years, however, and contemporary anthropologists continue to disagree about how it should be defined. Major debates about the culture concept, however, can be connected to particular intellectual and social struggles in which anthropologists have been involved historically.

2.1 Culture Against Racism: The Early Twentieth Century

Culture gained power as an anthropological concept in the early decades of the discipline, around the turn of the twentieth century, in a social and scholarly context in which all important differences between human groups were attributed to differences in the *biology* of the groups, summarized in the concept of *race*. Biological race was thought to be an infallible index for everything else distinctive to a particular human group. Many early physical anthropologists hoped that if they could succeed in accurately identifying the "races of Man," they would be able to specify which languages and customs originated with, belonged to, or were otherwise appropriate for which races. Unfortunately, this search for a scientific definition of race took place in a historical context in which ruling groups in the societies from which the anthropologists came were already convinced of the reality of race and so used race-based distinctions to justify their own domination of darker-skinned peoples around the globe.

In this context, the culture concept was a crucial innovation designed to counteract the racism implicit in nineteenth-century physical anthropology and, more broadly, in nineteenth-century social thought. At the turn of the twentieth century, under the influence of Franz Boas (1858–1942), anthropologists were collecting evidence to show that the diverse beliefs and practices that distinguished different groups of human beings from one another were due to differences in *social learning,* not differences in racial biology. For example, immigrants in the United States were assigned by physical anthropologists to a variety of different "races." Yet Boas and his colleagues were able to show that American-born children of immigrants regularly spoke fluent English, wore the clothing, ate the food, and otherwise adopted ways of life common in the United States. Boas even showed that the head shapes of the children of immigrants differed from the head shapes of their parents, apparently under the influence of nutritional changes. *Children in variation to parents*

The so-called races of Man were, in actuality, a single *human* race (or as we would say today, populations of a single human species). As a consequence, all were equipped with the same "pan-human rationality" and were equally capable of creating new cultural traits or adopting cultural traits from others. Another way to emphasize the equal humanity of all human groups was to demonstrate that each of them possessed the same kinds of institutions, or cultural universals, designed to achieve the same overall goals for the group's members. This was the path taken by Polish-British anthropologist Bronislaw Malinowski (1884–1942), who argued that all human beings everywhere face the same problems of survival or, as he put it, experience the same basic human needs. *all humans face the same problems* The members of each society use culture to devise ways of meeting these needs—for food or clothing or shelter or education or reproduction. Different societies meet these needs in different ways, however, and it is the ethnographer's job to catalogue the variety.

Boasians chose a different line of attack, arguing that race, language, and culture were independent phenomena. To show this was to show that the concept of biological race corresponded to no material reality and, thus, explained nothing about variation across human groups. That is, a person's physical attributes—skin color, hair texture, nose shape, stature, or the like—in no way compelled that person to speak or behave in any particular way. Indeed, the rapidity with which people of all "races" could forget old languages and customs and adopt new ones demonstrated the superiority of the culture concept in explaining variation across human groups. Since the capacities to create and learn culture belong to the entire human species, nothing prevents any subgroup from learning languages or beliefs or practices originally developed by some other subgroup.

Boas and his students devoted much effort to documenting an enormous amount of cultural borrowing across social, linguistic, and "racial" boundaries. This work aimed to demolish the concept of biological race for good, and yet at the beginning of the twenty-first century the concept of "race" has not disappeared. Indeed, the concept of culture explains how this can happen: people can invent *cultural* categories based on superficial physical features of human beings, call those categories "races," and then use these categories as building blocks for their social institutions, *even if such categories correspond to no biological reality.* An ongoing challenge within anthropology has been how to deny the reality of race as a biological concept without ignoring the continuing vigor of race as a cultural construction in societies like that of the United States.

Work by Boas and his students suggested strongly that the boundaries between various human groups are fuzzy and fluid and that firm distinctions are difficult to identify, let alone enforce. At the same time, it was apparent that different social groups often lived lives that were quite distinct from those of their neighbors, for several reasons. First, people did, initially at least, learn their native language and the bulk of their culture from those among whom they grew up. Second, social groups often deliberately emphasized unique cultural attributes in order to set themselves apart from their neighbors. Third, many of the groups ethnographers studied had been incorporated into a colonial empire (as in Africa) or within the boundaries of a larger nation-state (as in the United States). In such situations, the sorting of peoples into named societies, each associated with its own way of life, was strongly encouraged by the ruling elites.

2.2 The Evolution of Culture

Anthropologists in the early twentieth century worked within a Darwinian framework and were aware of the discoveries about biological heredity being made by the new science of genetics. Rather than explaining cultural variation in genetic terms, however, they sought to show the adaptive evolutionary advantages that culture provided for the human species. This theme has been emphasized in recent years by anthropologists known as *cultural inheritance theorists,* who seek to show how the capacity for human culture could have arisen by natural selection. Compared even to our nearest primate relatives, we human beings seem to be born remarkably free of specific "survival instincts," or biological programming designed to secure food, shelter, and mates for us automatically. Instead, as Malinowski suggested, every human group apparently can invent (and modify) its own particular sets of learned cultural traditions in order to solve these problems. Thus, human beings must learn everything necessary to survive and thrive from older, experienced members of their group. In Darwinian terms, they adapt to their environments by learning the culture of those among whom they live.

Such a form of Darwinian adaptation is highly unusual, however. How could it have arisen, and what would be the selective advantage for a species that relied on learned traditions, rather than innate biological programming, for survival? The anthropological answer goes something like this. Human beings are unusually intelligent (witness our large and complex brain). We and our ancestors ranged widely across many different kinds of natural environments, rather than being highly adapted to the resources of a narrow ecological niche, as, for example, are bamboo-eating giant pandas or eucalyptus-leaf-eating koalas. Natural selection for cultural learning in such an intelligent, wide-ranging species might have been favored because it allowed for a much more rapid adaptation to new environmental conditions than does natural selection operating on genes.

For example, human beings were not obliged to wait until natural selection provided them with thick fur before they could survive in cold climates. Instead, they could rely on their cultural capacity to learn to control fire, make warm clothing from skins, invent ways of using cold-adapted plants and animals for food, and so forth. Under such conditions, natural selection would also have favored those human ancestors who learned especially easily from those around them and who were curious and creative in devising cultural solutions for new adaptive problems. Research into human prehistory strongly supports this view of human beings as a species of "weedy generalists," equipped by natural selection with a set of adaptive traits, including a dependence on culture, that has made it possible to survive and thrive in virtually any environment the earth has to offer.

2.3 Culture and Symbolism

Human beings, of course, are not the only animals in the world that learn. Several decades of research, for example, have shown that chimpanzees have invented simple practices of various kinds that other members of their groups acquire through learning, such as fishing for termites with twigs, making leaf sponges to soak up water to drink, cracking nuts open with rocks, and assuming distinctive postures for grooming one another. If culture is defined as practices that are acquired from and shared with other members of one's social group, that mediate one's adaptation to the environment, and that get passed on from generation to generation by means of social learning, then these ape practices certainly can be called culture. At the same time, missing from these forms of ape culture is a key element that is integral to human culture. Unlike the learned behavior of other primates such as chimpanzees, human culture clearly depends on our use of **symbols**.

A symbol is something that stands for something else: "X symbolizes Y." What makes symbols distinct from other forms of representation is that there is *no necessary link* between the symbol (X) and that which it stands for (Y). Put another way, the relationship between a symbol and that which it stands for is conventional and arbitrary. Apes such as chimpanzees and bonobos do seem to have some rudimentary symbolic capacities, although just how much remains controversial. Nevertheless, these apes do not depend on symbolism to anything like the degree that human beings do. Thus, although learning is not unique to human beings and some learning of shared traditional practices can be found in nonhuman animals, only with human beings do we find a species whose survival depends on its reliance on learned, shared traditions that are *symbolically encoded.*

To depend on symbolic culture is to depend on learning for survival, but it is also much more. Symbols stand for objects, events, and processes in the wider world. But because their link to these phenomena is purely by convention, that which the symbol stands for can never be specified once and for all. The "same" phenomena may be symbolized differently in different societies, or phenomena that are distinguished as "different" in one society may be grouped together as instances of the "same" thing in another. This slippage between symbols and what they stand for makes possible complex human cultural systems, and it enables their remodeling or dismantling under novel conditions. Such slippage also means, however, that effort is constantly required to keep symbolic systems *systemic*—that is, orderly and coherent. Furthermore, nothing guarantees that existing cultural systems will not change over time, due either to internally generated developments or to exposure to new phenomena introduced from outside. *Cultural changes*

2.4 Ethnocentrism and Cultural Relativism

Still, despite these factors, ethnographers were impressed early on by the high degree of cultural coherence and predictability they regularly encountered while doing field research in non-Western cultures. This was important, because it undermined the racist stereotypes about tribal or non-Western peoples widespread in the

early decades of the discipline. In particular, such peoples were
regularly portrayed as irrational "savages" or "barbarians" leading lives that were, in the words of seventeenth-century philosopher Thomas Hobbes, "nasty, brutish, and short." Such portray-
als of tribal peoples by Western observers were based on the
universal human tendency to view one's own way of life as natural
and as naturally better than other, different ways of life. Anthropologists call this attitude ethnocentrism—that is, using the practices of your own "people" as a yardstick to measure how well the
customs of other, different peoples measure up. Inevitably, the
ways in which "they" differ from "us" (no matter who "they"
and "us" happen to be) are understood, ethnocentrically, in terms
of *what they lack.*

Bias

Ethnocentric Europeans and North Americans believed that to
be "civilized" and "cultured" meant to follow an orderly way of
life graced by refinement and harmony. But early anthropologists
found that they could use the culture concept to counter these ethnocentric beliefs. They could show that *all* peoples were equally
"cultured," because every group's social practices were characterized by order, harmony, and refinement. The particular set of customs one followed depended on the group one was born into,
from whose members one learned those customs. Another group's
customs might differ from our customs, but each group equally
had its own orderly, refined sets of customs. Thus, the child of an
aristocratic European family, if brought up among people who
hunted and gathered for a living, would learn the language and
culture of hunters and gatherers just as easily as one of their children, adopted by the aristocrats, would learn the language and
culture proper to aristocratic Europeans. To emphasize that every
society (not merely Western European society) had its own integrated culture was a way of emphasizing that each society was
human in its own way—indeed, that all human societies were
equally human.

The term *culture* came refer to a coherent set of beliefs and
customs belonging to a distinct society. Such a view seemed to
entail, at the very least, that those who were outsiders to someone
else's culture ought to refrain from assuming that difference auto-

ex. of fieldwork

matically meant inferiority. A culture could not be fully appreciated, anthropologists argued, until its various beliefs and practices were seen from the point of view of those who lived their lives according to those beliefs and practices. Ethnographic fieldwork introduced anthropologists to peoples about whom they previously lacked firsthand knowledge. By living side by side with people with an unfamiliar set of beliefs and practices for an extended period of time and learning the local language, anthropologists might hope to get a sense of what the world looked like from their hosts' point of view. This perspective on other cultures developed into the position called cultural relativism, whereby anthropologists were urged to interpret specific beliefs and practices in the context of the culture to which they belonged. More broadly, anthropologists urged others not to make snap judgments about the value of other peoples' customs but to consider first the role those customs fulfilled within the culture in which they were found. Cultural relativism gave anthropologists (and the members of the societies they studied) ideological ammunition to use against missionaries or colonialists who felt no compunction whatsoever about moving into "primitive" societies and destroying indigenous customs that were not to their liking.

In this sense, cultural anthropologists in the first half of the twentieth century believed that the ethnographic evidence they collected in societies throughout the world supported their claims of equal capacity and equal dignity for all human beings. Knowledge of the orderly, predictable customs and practices characteristic of tribal peoples became well known in Western circles, largely thanks to the work of anthropologists like Margaret Mead (1901–78) in the United States and Malinowski in Britain, who communicated anthropological findings through popular media to a wide audience outside university circles.

Still, not everyone was persuaded by their views. Indeed, new stereotypes about "primitive peoples" emerged that took account of anthropological evidence. It no longer seemed plausible to claim that "savages" and "barbarians" were wild, unruly, and irrational. And so ethnocentric Europeans and North Americans began to argue that "they" were different from "us" because of

"racist" remarks grew

"their" slavish obedience to tradition, their mindless and uncriti-
cal repetition of traditions they'd inherited from their ancestors.
People in "modern" Western societies with "scientific" cultures,
by contrast, were portrayed as both able and willing to question
the validity and rationality of traditional practices and to replace
outmoded customs with better-adapted innovations. To view culture as a prison house of custom from which non-Western and
tribal peoples were powerless to escape on their own, however,
was to take the anthropological concept of culture and apply it in
ways that the anthropologists who first developed it had never
intended.

2.5 The Boundaries of Culture?

After World War II, European imperial power declined, former
colonies were transformed into independent states, and the Civil
Rights movement in the United States began to gather momentum. In the context of so many social, cultural, and political
changes, and so many challenges to previous authority, the
anthropological portrait of a world made up of particular mutually exclusive societies, each with its own, internally consistent
culture, increasingly came under scrutiny, both within and outside
anthropology.

Some anthropologists had always raised questions about just
how sharply bounded, just how internally integrated, any particular culture might be. Boas and his students, as noted previously,
had documented much borrowing of cultural objects and practices by one supposedly distinct society from another, suggesting
that boundaries between cultural traditions might be rather
porous. But if society A borrowed a custom from society B, could
that custom ever be made into an "authentic" part of the culture
of society A? And if it could be integrated, did that mean that the
culture of society A was no longer "authentic"? And who would
decide? Furthermore, even if a provisional correspondence could
be established between a particular society and a particular set of
cultural beliefs and practices, was it plausible to claim that every
member of that society shared *every* aspect of its culture—the
same beliefs, the same values, the same practices, the same points

[handwritten marginal note: people began to view culture as a type of prison.]

of view? What if members of the society in question disagreed, say, about how to perform a ritual? Could only one of the parties be correct, and must the others necessarily be wrong? And, again, who would decide?

Ethnographers often sought research settings that seemed to approximate this ideal of cultural uniformity—for example, remote villages or culturally distinct urban neighborhoods. Often they had to acknowledge that this setting was only one part of a larger sociocultural system, even if that larger system was not the focus of their research. This was particularly visible, and problematic, in the case of ethnographic work carried out during the colonial period: the wider imperial setting would be acknowledged briefly, but little or no reference to that setting would be made in the rest of the ethnography.

In recent years, many anthropologists have begun to question the validity of speaking as if a large and complex society could possess a single, uniform "culture." It has also become obvious that even within relatively small homogenous societies, members may disagree with one another about what "their culture" actually is. Anthropologists have become increasingly sensitive to the political issues involved in drawing boundaries around a society or a culture or in taking the views of one subgroup of a larger society as representative of "the culture" as a whole. This is why contemporary anthropologists always acknowledge that social and cultural boundaries are not eternally fixed and why they explicitly question, rather than assume they already know, what any particular set of boundaries means.

2.6 The Concept of Culture in a Global World: Problems and Practices

This has led to rethinking of the way ethnography should be pursued in a world in which local conditions are never isolated from global forces. One solution is to undertake what has been called *multisited ethnography*: doing fieldwork not only in a particular local setting (a small village, say) but also in a series of other settings (such as political or corporate centers, whether in the same country or abroad). For example, fieldwork might begin in an urban neighborhood in the United States among a group of immigrants from elsewhere. But it might extend into the urban and national bureaucratic settings in which decisions affecting the immigrant group are made, and it might even continue in the communities abroad from which the immigrants originally came. The advantages and disadvantages of multisited ethnography are still being debated, but the fact that such a research strategy exists testifies to anthropologists' awareness of the often wide-ranging network of complex forces in which any particular local community is enmeshed.

Similarly, contemporary ethnographies are often quite explicit about exactly which members of a group have provided cultural information about a particular issue. Thus, anthropologists are careful to distinguish the opinions of, say, older men from those of women or of younger men, because they have learned that these subgroups regularly have differential access to social power and different interests to defend and so have different interpretations to offer about the cultural institutions and practices in which they are involved.

With this new awareness has come the realization that a concept of culture that emphasizes uniformity of belief and practice is not only not always liberating but can also be used as a way of enforcing inequality. This is clearest when one subgroup within a larger society insists on its version of the tradition as the only correct version and tries to force other subgroups to profess allegiance to that version or else risk persecution. Such practices are perhaps most obvious in those societies that were once colonies but have since become independent states. A common experience in such new states was the discovery that very little, apart from joint opposition to the colonizing power, united the peoples who were citizens of these new states. The ruling groups who had inherited the reins of government following the departure of the colonizer all felt very strongly the need to build some kind of national unity based on a shared "national culture." But the elements of such a national culture could be difficult to find when the only historical experience shared by all the new citizens was the tradition of colonial domination. Sometimes appeal could be made to precolonial customs—religious, economic, or political practices, for example—that were distinct from those that had been introduced by the colonial power. If such practices had once been widely shared, or at least widely recognized, by the bulk of the population, they might become resources on which to build a new national identity. If, however, such practices belonged only to a tiny proportion of the new citizenry—perhaps a powerful tribal group that had come to dominate postcolonial politics, for example—the practices might well be resisted by other groups. Having expelled one colonial power, they would see no advantage in being recolonized by one of their neighbors.

Paradoxically, however, elements of colonial culture often played an important role in the construction of the new national culture. This included not only the bureaucratic apparatus of governmental administration inherited from the colonial past and the new ways of doing business or educating the young introduced during the colonial period but also the language in which all these activities would be carried out. Anthropologists studying the production of national culture have been influenced by the writings of political scientist Benedict Anderson, who argued that nation-states are "imagined communities," most of whose members never see one another face-to-face but who nonetheless experience a sense of fellow feeling for one another. In Anderson's view, much of that fellow feeling in new nation-states develops out of their members' shared experiences of colonial institutions and practices.

Once again, language is a good example. If the peoples who were administered within a single colony came from dozens or hundreds of different ethnic groups, speaking numerous mutually unintelligible languages, any shared sense of belonging to the same nation would likely be very slight. However, once children from all those different groups began to attend colonial schools and learn the colonizer's language, they did have things in common. Moreover, they could then speak with and learn about one another in a way that would not have been possible had they not all learned to speak, say, French in French colonial schools. Again and again, the new nation-states chose the language of their former colonizer as the new national language of government, business, and education. Not only was this "efficient" in that it allowed an important element of continuity in changing circumstances, but it also meant that the official language of the state did not favor any particular indigenous language group over the others.

The culture concept thus can be reformulated to describe an emerging national culture, and attempts can be made to relate that national culture to the local cultures of different groups incorporated within the nation-state. What anthropologists did not expect, however, and what led to their most serious questioning of the traditional culture concept, were cases in which national regimes in various countries did not recognize the existence within their borders of such differentiated and partially overlapping cultures. Thus, if outsiders objected to the way a particular regime was treating its own citizens, spokespersons for the regime might respond that such treatment was "part of their culture" and, as such, beyond the critique of outsiders whose cultures were different. Most notoriously, under apartheid in South Africa, it was official government policy to endorse the notion that each people had its own unique culture. The apartheid regime assigned indigenous African peoples to "homelands" in rural areas far from mines and farms and factories, on the dubious grounds that Africans properly belonged in rural areas, farming the way their ancestors had done, and were not suited to work in, let alone run, modern commercial or industrial institutions in South Africa, because these institutions were part of "European culture."

2.7 Culture: Contemporary Discussion and Debate

What has been the outcome of all this discussion and debate about the culture concept? Some anthropologists assert that the concept of culture has been forever tainted by the older usage that assigned every society its own unique, internally harmonious set of beliefs and practices. Because this use of the concept reflects an outmoded understanding of how societies and cultures relate to one another, they argue, and has permitted culture to be falsely understood as a prison house of custom from which people could never escape, the term should be discarded entirely. They believe that it bears too many traces of the colonial circumstances under which it was developed and to which it proved so useful an intellectual tool in dividing and dominating colonized peoples.

But abandoning the one-society-one-culture model does not mean that the concept of culture needs to be discarded. Many of the anthropologists who reject that model prefer to think of culture as the sum total of all the customs and practices humans have ever produced. They point out that, with the increasing speed and density of communication and travel, nobody anywhere on the face of the earth is isolated from the major flows of information and activity present in our contemporary world. Fast food, rock music, and computers have a worldwide appeal. Because we are a species that needs to learn how to survive and are willing to learn new things from others, people everywhere now seem to be involved in stitching together their own patchwork of beliefs and practices from both local traditions and the wide range of global culture locally available. In situations like this, many contemporary anthropologists argue that what counts as anyone's culture is "up for grabs."

And yet those processes that turn culture into something individuals put together on their own are frequently countered by another process in which groups defend a uniform and closed view of their own culture in the face of potential inundation by global culture. Thus, much like some early anthropologists, contemporary activists in movements of ethnic solidarity defend a monolithic, internally harmonious view of their own culture against "outside" forces claiming to know what is best for them. Such a defense, however, is not without its own paradoxes. For example, in order to present the image of a united front, ethnic activists must downplay the same kinds of internal divisions and disagreements that anthropologists have been criticized for ignoring in traditional ethnographies that emphasize cultural uniformity. Activists may be fully aware of this paradox but still believe that it is justified for political reasons.

At the same time, some individuals defend their right to pick and choose from global culture the customs they want to follow and resist attempts by other members of groups to which they belong to police their beliefs and behavior. More than that, they may challenge those who criticize them for incorporating borrowed cultural practices alongside those they have inherited, asserting that theirs is a living cultural tradition and all living cultural traditions will sometimes change in this way. They insist that the end result need not be "Westernization" or "Americanization" of their own cultures; rather, they speak of the "Africanization" or "Botswanization" or "Ju/'hoansization"—that is, the indigenization—of cultural features that may have originated in the West or in America but have been adopted by local people for local purposes. Because these outside cultural elements are chosen by insiders rather than imposed by outsiders, they are seen to enrich, rather than to destroy or replace, the cultural traditions into which they are being integrated. Prior to the end of the twentieth century, for example, literacy may not have been part of the cultural heritage of southern African foragers like the Ju/'hoansi. But many contemporary Ju/'hoansi who have learned to read and write and transcribe their own language view these as positive changes that strengthen their ongoing, developing cultural tradition. Picking up on these developments, some anthropologists are paying renewed attention to the kinds of cultural borrowing highlighted by the Boasians a century ago, but with a twist. In the contemporary context, anthropologists take for granted that all living cultural traditions are dynamic and open to change. As a result, they draw attention to the deliberation and choice exercised by members of these societies who selectively adopt elements of other cultures, not as a way of rejecting their own tradition for an alien alternative, but in order to reaffirm and strengthen their own evolving cultural identity.

2.8 Culture: A Contemporary Consensus

If there is a contemporary anthropological consensus about the nature of culture, it would seem to involve at least the four following propositions. First, nobody questions that culture is learned, not genetically programmed. Second, many anthropologists would argue that the kind of culture that is learned (and the way it is learned) is never innocent but is always shaped by power relations of some kind. Third, power relations and cultural forms that are global in scope have penetrated local communities and local cultures; the ultimate consequences for anybody's culture are still to be assessed. But fourth, it is incorrect to assume that the penetration of local communities by global culture dooms all local cultural traditions to extinction. On the contrary, local societies can and do indigenize cultural elements that arrive from elsewhere, regularly subverting their homogenizing or "Westernizing" potential and putting them to work in ways that preserve and enhance local goals and interests.

2.9 Summary

In this chapter, we looked at the history of the concept of culture in anthropology and the way it has been defined in recent years. We considered the ways in which the concept of culture has been used and its connection with ethnocentrism and cultural relativism. Finally, we examined the ways in which particular historical contexts and political concerns may shape the way in which the term culture is used.

For Further Reading

IDEAS OF CULTURE
Bohannan 1995; Gamst and Norbeck 1976

CONTEMPORARY CRITIQUES
Anderson 1983; Clifford 1988; Hannerz 1996; Marcus and Fischer 1986

THE CONCEPT OF RACE
Contemporary Issues Forum 1998

APE CULTURE
Savage-Rumbaugh et al. 1986

3
Language

The key terms and concepts covered in this chapter, in the order in which they appear:

language
linguistics
anthropological
    linguistics
linguistic anthropology

protolanguage
language family

ethnolinguistics

diachronic
synchronic
historical linguistics

grammar
paralanguage
kinesics
code
openness
phonology
phonemes
phonetics

morpheme
morphology

syntagmatic
form class
paradigmatic
frame substitution
syntax
surface structure
deep structure

semantics
linguistic competence
linguistic performance
communicative
    competence
Sapir-Whorf hypothesis
ethnosemantics
ethnoscience
etic
emic

speech community
regional dialects
social dialects
registers

sociolinguistics
verbal repertoire
code-switching
diglossia

discourse

pragmatics
ethnopragmatics

pidgin
creole
linguistic nationalism

HUMAN BEINGS, ALONE AMONG all living species, rely on spoken language to communicate with one another. This fact has puzzled and intrigued people in all societies, has played an important role in religious and philosophical reflections on the human condition, and has been a central focus of attention in anthropology from the very beginning. Trying to define language in a clear and unambiguous way, however, has proved surprisingly difficult. Today, most anthropologists would probably agree, minimally, that **language** is a system of arbitrary vocal symbols that human beings use to encode their experience of the world and to communicate with one another. The scholarly discipline that pursues a scientific study of language is called **linguistics.** The terms **anthropological linguistics** and **linguistic anthropology** have been used by anthropologists to refer to the study of language in cultural context.

3.1 Studying Language: A Historical Sketch

The study of language was central to early anthropology because it was a dimension of culture that was easy to observe and study in detail. For example, languages (like the cultures in which they are embedded) show tremendous variation, both over time and across space. The European study of systematic linguistic change over time is usually said to have begun with the work of the British scholar Sir William Jones (1746–94), who studied Sanskrit in India. He pointed out in 1786 that Sanskrit, classical Greek, Latin, and more recent European languages shared numerous similarities, suggesting that they may have all diverged from a common ancestral language, or **protolanguage,** that came to be called *Indo-European.* All languages believed to have descended from a common ancestral language are said to belong to the same **language family.** By 1822, the German scholar Jakob Grimm (of fairy tale fame; 1785–1863) was able to show that regular changes in speech sounds could be traced over succeeding generations of speakers of a single language or among speakers of related languages as they diverged.

In the twentieth century, linguistic anthropologists have been interested in the ways that linguistic change often is triggered by unpredictable and unforeseen cultural and historical events, rather than being generated solely within language itself. The long-standing anthropological focus on the relation between language and culture is sometimes referred to as **ethnolinguistics.**

A major shift in the scholarly approach to language study occurred early in the twentieth century, when scholars turned their attention from studies of language that were **diachronic** (concerned with change over time) to studies of language that were **synchronic** (concerned with the patterns present in a particular language at a particular point in time). The terms *synchronic* and *diachronic* were invented early in the twentieth century by the Swiss scholar Ferdinand de Saussure (1857–1913), one of the architects of this transformation. And from Saussure's time onward, scholars involved in synchronic language studies became known as *linguists*—distinct from *philologists,* who retained a focus on reconstructing linguistic divergence, primarily from written texts. Interest in language history did not disappear, but, influenced by the orientation and practices of scholars like Saussure, it became known as **historical linguistics.** Finally, followers of Saussure called themselves *descriptive* linguists, since their goal was to describe the rules that governed language as people actually spoke it; they contrasted this goal with that of old-fashioned *prescriptive* grammarians, who saw their job as correcting ordinary speech to make it conform to some ideal literary model of proper grammatical usage.

As noted previously, defining language has always been difficult, primarily because it has so many dimensions to which attention might be directed. First, people frequently communicate successfully with one another without using language. Second, people can use language to communicate without actually speaking (they can use gestures or exchange written messages, for example). Linguists traditionally have focused on spoken language, showing how human speech sounds can be grouped into recurring sequences, often called *words,* which are combined into longer utterances according to specific rules. The elements of language and rules for combining words are generally referred to as **grammar.** But much besides grammar is associated with spoken language, such as the various qualities with which we utter our words (volume, pitch, emphasis, speed, and so forth), which linguists call **paralanguage.**

Moreover, grammar and paralanguage do not contain all the meaning we convey when we speak; meaning is also carried by such things as our postures, our facial expressions, and our accompanying gestures. These phenomena, which are sometimes called *body language,* have been studied by anthropologists using a special system of notation called **kinesics.** In addition, we often choose our words carefully, depending on the person we are addressing or the setting in which we are speaking, which highlights the important role context plays in shaping the meaning of our utterances. Finally, as the philologists showed, the language our grandparents (or more distant ancestors) used often differs markedly from the language we use today. So how much of all this should we take into consideration when we study language?

To answer this question, Saussure made an important distinction between what came out of people's mouths when they spoke (which he called *parole*) and the underlying rules that generated that speech (which he called *langue*). In his view, parole varied from speaker to speaker, reflecting each individual's idiosyncratic interests and stylistic preferences, whereas langue referred to the stable, universal rules that all speakers observed. Saussure wanted to define language in a way that would permit him to study it scientifically. Therefore, he recommended paying attention only to the most systematic and unvarying elements of language—that is, to langue, which corresponds to what other linguists call the linguistic **code** or grammar. Saussure argued that langue (the code or grammar shared by all speakers) was a self-contained system and that the significance of any element in the system (such as sounds or words) depended on its relationship with other elements in the system, rather than on some feature of the outside world.

Saussure's approach to language had at least two major consequences. First, it gave linguists a clear-cut object of study, whose intricate details they could probe without distraction; the end result was the birth of the independent discipline of linguistics, which continues this investigation today. Second, it drew attention to the *arbitrariness* of the relationship between the sounds (or words) of language, the meanings they stood for, and the objects in the world to which they referred. Saussure showed convincingly that the sounds of language, by themselves, carried no inherent meaning: a flat-topped piece of furniture with four legs called "table" in English is called "mesa" in Spanish. Subsequent anthropological linguists, like Charles Hockett, would argue that the arbitrariness of the link between sound and meaning in human language was one of a number of related *design features* of language. Furthermore, they would argue that this arbitrariness was a consequence of the design feature Hockett called **openness,** the possibility of using the linguistic code to create totally new combinations of elements in order to articulate meanings never before uttered.

Along with Saussure, Franz Boas often is credited with contributing to the birth of modern linguistics and linguistic anthropology. His focus on language developed as he sought a way of studying culture in a detailed and nuanced way. It seemed clear to him, as it did to other ethnographers of his generation, like Bronislaw Malinowski, that a profound understanding of another culture could not be gained unless the ethnographer knew the language used by members of that culture to articulate their understandings of the world and of themselves. Boas's own observations about language, based on his field experiences, also drew attention to the codelike fashion in which languages were organized.

3.2 The Building Blocks of Language

One tradition of linguistic scholarship that can be traced back to the influence of Boas and Saussure focused on linguistic codes themselves. Early linguists were especially interested in the sound patterns peculiar to particular languages, an area of linguistics that came to be called **phonology.** An important early discovery was that every language has a restricted set of sounds that are recognized by all native speakers and that can be combined according to rules to form all the words of the language. These minimal units of sound recognized by speakers of a particular language, called **phonemes,** are contrasted with the much larger range of speech sounds human beings are theoretically capable of producing and hearing, the scientific study of which is called **phonetics.**

Many early linguists analyzed the sets of phonemes characteristic of particular languages. They were also interested in minimal units of meaning in languages. Although in languages like English such units often correspond to *words,* comparative work in very different languages, such as those of indigenous Americans, demonstrated that not all languages are put together the way English is. And so linguists adopted a new term, **morpheme,** to refer to the minimal unit of meaning in a language and studied the rules for combining morphemes in a branch of linguistics known as **morphology.**

In the first half of the twentieth century, linguists thought of grammar as having two kinds of elements, phonemes and morphemes, each with its own particular set of rules for combination. Following Saussure, these linguists used two procedures to identify rules for combining morphemes. Working with native speakers, they collected texts in the language being studied and examined them for regularities. Saussure conceived of these regularities as falling along two intersecting axes, one vertical and one horizontal. The horizontal, or **syntagmatic,** axis was used to plot the linearity of speech, and many utterances were compared to isolate those grammatical units (traditionally called *parts of speech*) that worked the same way in all utterances. Once the grammatical units had been identified, linguists could then work out which morphemes in the language functioned as which grammatical units. All the morphemes that could substitute for one another at a particular point in the syntagmatic sequence (or sentence) were said to belong to the same **form class** and could be arranged along a vertical, or **paradigmatic,** axis. By leaving a space in the syntagmatic sequence where that form class normally occurred and by asking native speakers of the language which morphemes might properly fill that space, linguists could isolate all the members of a particular form class, a procedure called **frame substitution.** For example, in English, the utterance "The tourist _____ along the sidewalk" is a syntagmatic substitution frame, and all the English words that fit into the empty slot (e.g., *walked, ran,* or *strolled*) belong to the same form class—that is, verbs. All the verbs (including these three) that correctly fill the empty slot of this substitution frame can be aligned along a vertical paradigmatic axis as options that may be grammatically substituted for one another as the speaker chooses.

Working out the syntagmatic structure characteristic of a particular language and using that structure to create substitution frames for eliciting the members of paradigmatic form classes provided a powerful way for descriptive linguists to highlight key features of any language's grammar. But phonological and morphological rules alone could not account for the features of all grammatical sentences, a point forcefully made in 1957 by Noam Chomsky. Chomsky argued that sentences were themselves units of grammatical structure, and he proposed that linguists begin to study **syntax,** the structure of sentences. Chomsky suggested that syntactic relationships could be explained if it were recognized that sentences could be analyzed at two levels: in terms of surface structure and deep structure. **Surface structure** was what came out of people's mouths when they spoke and was the level of structure traditionally studied by descriptive linguists. However, surface structure exhibited a number of peculiarities that could not be explained in terms of the linear sequence of grammatical units and substitutions.

For example, Chomsky observed that native speakers of English were convinced that sentences like "A woman won the contest" and "The contest was won by a woman" were related to one another; grammarians might say they were two versions of a single sentence, the first in active voice and the second in passive voice. Chomsky's syntactic theory built on this intuition of relatedness by claiming that both surface versions of the sentence shared the same **deep structure** and that the passive surface structure was the outcome of the application of a syntactic rule (called the *passive transformation rule*) to the underlying deep syntactic structure of the sentence.

Chomsky later argued that any grammar ought to be a theory of a language, and since all languages were used to convey meanings, every grammar ought to contain a component concerned with how that language dealt with meaning. This justified attention to **semantics,** or the study of meaning, a dimension of language that traditionally had been viewed as too vague and variable to serve as an object of linguistic investigation. The fields of formal syntax and semantics have developed in different directions since the 1960s, but all those developments have roots in the initial orientations provided by Chomsky.

When Chomsky distinguished between deep structure and surface structure, he was building on Saussure's distinction between langue and parole. Like langue, deep structure referred to the stable, unvarying rules of grammar observed by all native speakers of a language; by contrast, like parole, surface structure supposedly varied from speaker to speaker in an unpredictable way. Chomsky also observed that people's actual utterances often were full of errors, hesitations, and false starts that might be the result of physical factors such as sleepiness and thus did not truly represent their underlying grammatical knowledge. And so Chomsky further distinguished between **linguistic competence** (the underlying knowledge of grammatical rules encoded in the brains of all fluent speakers of a language) and **linguistic performance** (the actual things people said, which for the reasons mentioned, might not reflect their actual linguistic competence). Much like Saussure, Chomsky thought linguists should ignore linguistic performance and try to develop theories of linguistic competence.

3.3 Language and Culture

Chomsky's influence in linguistics was nothing short of revolutionary, and it accentuated a split between those linguists who focused on the code alone and other students of language who remained concerned with how speakers used the code in different cultural and social settings. The anthropological linguist Dell Hymes summarized the objections of this latter group when he compared Chomsky's notion of linguistic competence to his own concept of **communicative competence.** Chomsky's focus on the linguistic code led him to define linguistic competence in terms of a speaker's knowledge of the difference between grammatical and ungrammatical sentences in a language.

But Hymes pointed out that successful use of language to communicate with other people requires far more than just grammatical knowledge. It requires speakers to choose vocabulary and topics of speech that are suitable to different audiences in different social settings. For example, fluent speakers of a language might show linguistic competence in their use of casual, grammatically correct linguistic forms in their conversations with friends. But they would betray a colossal lack of communicative competence if they used the same forms when introducing a visiting foreign dignitary in a formal public setting. To identify what constitutes communicative competence, researchers must pay attention to parole, to surface structure, and to actual linguistic performance. According to anthropological linguists like Hymes, these phenomena are not wholly idiosyncratic but show far more culturally shaped regularity than the followers of Saussure or Chomsky have ever acknowledged.

At midcentury, Hymes represented a second tradition of scholarship on language that could be traced back to Boas. Practitioners in this tradition continued to see the study of a particular linguistic code primarily as a means to a more profound understanding of culture, rather than as an end in itself. After Boas, in the 1920s and 1930s, the best-known proponents of this approach were Edward Sapir and Benjamin Whorf. Both were struck by the ways in which linguistic form and cultural meaning shaped each other, and each in his own way tried to characterize that relationship. Whorf's analyses of the grammatical codes of indigenous North American languages like Hopi attracted attention (and eventual notoriety) both within and outside anthropology. In several controversial articles, he seemed to be claiming that every language had a unique, self-contained grammar that strongly influenced the thought patterns and cultural practices of its speakers.

After World War II, when both Sapir and Whorf were dead, other anthropologists, linguists, and psychologists tried to devise experiments that would test the influence of language on culture and thought. These researchers advanced what they called the **Sapir-Whorf hypothesis:** the claim that the culture and thought patterns of people were strongly influenced by the language they spoke. Immediately, however, the researchers faced a familiar problem: How do you define "language" and "culture" and "thought" with sufficient rigor so that it becomes possible to measure the degree to which one does or does not influence the other(s)? In practice, "language" was equated with "grammatical code," and tests were devised to measure whether speakers whose grammars possessed (or lacked) certain grammatical structures were correspondingly forced to perceive (or prevented from perceiving) those structures when they looked at the world around them. For example, does an absence of grammatical marking on verbs for past, present, and future tense mean that speakers of that language cannot perceive the passage of time? Or, if a language has only three terms for basic colors (e.g., *black, white,* and *red*), does this mean that speakers of that language cannot tell the difference between the colors an English speaker identifies as *green* and *blue*?

Actual research showed that questions posed in this fashion were far too simplistic, both about grammars and about human perception. Any language is always a part of some culture—that is, it is learned, not innate, and it is intimately interrelated with all cultural practices in which its speakers engage—and thinking cannot easily be distinguished from the linguistic and cultural activity in which it is regularly involved. Thus, it is virtually impossible to tease language, culture, and thought apart, let alone to figure out the direction of the causal arrows that supposedly link them to one another. By the early 1960s, most anthropological linguists had concluded that there was no solid evidence that grammatical features of particular languages *determined* thought patterns or cultural practices. The fact that many people throughout the world were bi- or multilingual, successfully communicating with speakers of languages with sometimes very different grammatical codes (e.g., Hopi and English), called into question the supposition that people typically were monolingual—that is, they knew or spoke fluently only one language from birth to death.

In the 1950s and 1960s, a number of anthropologists developed a research program known as **ethnosemantics** or **ethnoscience** that aimed for greater accuracy and sophistication. As the labels suggest, their goal was to discover the systems of linguistic meaning and classification developed by people in their own languages and used in their own cultures. Borrowing the linguistic contrast between phonetic and phonemic studies of the sounds of language, ethnoscientists explicitly contrasted **etic** categories devised by outside researchers and **emic** categories devised by native speaker-informants. Their goal was to describe as faithfully as possible the emic categories used by informants in their own language, and so they encouraged a rigorous set of research practices involving substitution frames in order to protect their data from etic contamination.

For all their achievements, however, ethnoscientists continued to work with a theoretical model of language and culture in which researchers and informants were understood to belong to mutually exclusive monolingual and monocultural worlds. It was not that anthropologists failed to recognize the inaccuracy of the model. Fieldwork and study had made many of them bi- or multilingual and bi- or multicultural, and a history of colonial conquest followed by linguistic and cultural imperialism had often made many of their informants bi- or multicultural and bi- or multilingual as well.

3.4 Language and Society

The necessity of taking this bi- and multilingualism/culturalism into theoretical account prompted Hymes to urge his colleagues to move beyond the study of individual languages to the study of speech communities. A **speech community** is any concrete community of individuals who regularly interact verbally with one another. It might be a village or a neighborhood or a city; today it might include "virtual communities" created by Internet chat rooms or e-mail. Hymes pointed out that if you delimit a speech community and then do an inventory of all the different kinds of language used by members of that community, you will quickly discover not merely one version of one language in use, but rather a variety of forms of one language (and sometimes more than one language) in use. Some varieties will be **regional dialects:** versions of a particular language associated with particular geographical settings, such as the Appalachian versus Texan versus New England dialects of North American English. Some will be **social dialects:** versions of a particular language associated with particular social groups, such as the "Cockney" working-class dialect of London as contrasted with the "BBC English" of the educated British upper middle class. Still others will be social **registers:** versions of a particular language associated with particular social settings, such as a court of law or an elementary school playground or a house of religious worship. Every member of the speech community may not be able to converse fluently in all the varieties represented in the community, but all members will ordinarily have control of several varieties, each of which will be called for in a different set of circumstances.

This approach developed in anthropological linguistics by Hymes was supported by similar approaches developed in sociolinguistics by sociologists such as John Gumperz. **Sociolinguistics** is usually defined as the study of the relationship between language and society. Traditionally, it has been interested in correlations between social variation (e.g., class or ethnic stratification) and linguistic variation (e.g., in the form of regional or social dialects), as well as correlations between particular social settings and linguistic registers. Together, Gumperz and Hymes developed analytic concepts that meshed in interesting ways. For example, if every speech community is characterized by a number of different language varieties, then every member of that speech community can be described in terms of her or his **verbal repertoire:** the sum total of verbal varieties a particular individual has mastered.

Gumperz and others were able to show that the number and nature of the varieties within an individual's verbal repertoire not only offer a good set of indicators as to that individual's social identity and status but also are a good predictor of that individual's probable success in interacting verbally with speakers of different identities and statuses. Gumperz described verbal repertoires as sets of weapons that one could deploy in verbal (and social) struggles with others. Like soldiers with a range of weapons, people with more varieties in their repertoires could attain objectives in a range of social situations. They could switch from one variety (or code) to another as the situation demanded, a phenomenon called **code-switching.** Some sociolinguists have described speech communities in which everyone was fluent in two codes (either two dialects of a single language or two different languages), a phenomenon described as **diglossia.** Where diglossia occurs, speakers generally use each code in mutually exclusive settings (e.g., one at home and the other at school), switching back and forth between codes as the situation demands. One insight provided by studies of verbal repertoires is that speakers with fewer codes at their command are both socially and verbally limited in their interactions with others.

Hymes's suggestion that anthropological linguistics should focus on how people develop communicative competence in speech communities characterized by multiple codes stimulated research in a number of related areas. One was the comparative study of childhood acquisition of communicative competence, which involved mastering not only grammatical rules but also rules for appropriate use. Another was the study of classifications of forms of talk in specific cultures and examination of the various contexts in which these forms were used. A third was the study of culture-specific verbal performances like storytelling, in which the codes known by the storyteller and her or his listeners were resources upon which the storyteller could draw in exercising individual artistic agency.

Studies of verbal performance emphasized all those features of language that formal linguists ignored, such as figurative language, wordplay, deliberate rule-breaking and code-switching to achieve certain rhetorical effects. Anthropological linguists carrying out cross-cultural research on verbal performance were able to show that, however central the rules of grammar remain for effective linguistic communication, in real life, when people struggle to defend their interests using whatever tools are available, rules of grammar and rules of use can be bent or broken to achieve other communicative effects. And if rules can be broken, perhaps they are as much a product of other social and cultural communication as they are shapers of that communication.

The focus on multiple linguistic varieties present in all speech communities and on rules for their appropriate use inevitably drew attention to the fact that not all varieties were accorded equal respect and that most linguists who talk about "the" grammar of language X ordinarily had in mind only one high-prestige variety of language X. If they were, like Chomsky, educated linguists studying their own native language, the grammar in question was likely to be that language's literary standard, such as Standard English. And since native-speaker linguists were told to trust their own intuitions in deciding whether certain usages were "grammatical," it became increasingly clear that, in practice, "linguistic competence" meant competence in the standard variety. Despite linguists' assertions that their work was descriptive, not prescriptive, nonstandard varieties inevitably appeared ungrammatical with respect to the standard, making those varieties (and, by extension, their speakers) look defective.

3.5 Discourse

Such judgments looked suspiciously like the old-fashioned opinions of prescriptive grammarians. From the point of view of linguistic anthropologists, they reflected sociocultural evaluations of speakers associated with those linguistic varieties, evaluations that inevitably reflected the unequal power relations between evaluators and those being evaluated. Linguistic anthropologists began to focus explicitly on the way linguistic usage and evaluations of linguistic usage were shaped by power struggles between various subgroups within a society. They emphasized that rules of "grammaticality" or "cultural acceptability" often are based on linguistic forms preferred by powerful groups in society. As a result, disadvantaged groups may choose to express resistance against a given power structure by refusing to use the linguistic forms endorsed by the powerful. Some linguistic anthropologists have shown how this takes place in the course of public and private performances of different culturally recognized forms of **discourse** (talk), such as storytelling, oratory, popular theater, and traditional forms of poetic expression (e.g., funeral laments). Such work made very clear that those who engage in particular forms of discourse are not forced by rules of grammar or culture to say some things rather than others. Quite the opposite: they struggle to use the rules of grammar and culture as *resources* to convey their own, often subversive, messages to their audiences.

The focus of scholars like Hymes and Gumperz on speech communities whose members each possessed verbal repertoires consisting of multiple language varieties often was seen as a way of displaying the complexity and coordination of cultural and linguistic variation within a society. It also highlighted the sophistication with which people regularly matched appropriate forms of discourse to appropriate audiences or settings. Following the rise of postmodern critique in anthropology in the 1980s, however, attention began to shift to the prisonlike rules that aimed to constrain people's behavior and speech within particular limits and to the struggles in which people engaged to resist such limitation. In linguistic anthropology, this reorientation was assisted by the adoption of the concepts and approach of a group of Russian literary and linguistic scholars associated with Mikhail Bakhtin, whose key texts had recently been translated into English. Hymes and Gumperz's image of speech communities whose members made use of multiple varieties of languages was echoed in Bakhtin's concept of *heteroglossia*, or "many-voicedness," among speakers in a society. The emphasis of Bakhtin's discussion, however, was on how different groups of speakers, each rooted in their own particular (and unequal) positions within society, struggle for control of public discourse.

Linguistic anthropologists influenced by Bakhtin were particularly interested in the discourse of low-status groups that could not safely challenge those who dominated them in an open fashion. Bakhtin's concept of *double-voiced discourse* proved very useful, for it emphasized that the "same" words or expressions can mean different things to different speakers who use them in different contexts. Bakhtin was especially interested in the ironic use of language, in which listeners understand that words mean the opposite of what they ordinarily signify because of the context in which they are uttered, and in parodic language, in which officially acceptable language is exaggerated or mimicked with the intention of poking fun. Such forms of double-voiced discourse allow speakers to keep their actual words within acceptable grammatical and cultural boundaries, while elements of the context within which the words are spoken imparts to them a meaning quite different from their formal denotations. Officially, order is upheld, but unofficially, it is held up to ridicule or critique.

To focus on subversive forms of talk like double-voiced discourse is to emphasize the way in which language in cultural contexts of use twists and manipulates the supposedly unvarying and stable elements of formal grammar. The demonstration was so powerful that even formal linguists, working in the Chomskian tradition, had to take notice. They began to include a **pragmatics** component in their formal grammars, which purported to catalogue universal rules of use obeyed by all speakers of all languages who wanted to communicate successfully with others. Linguistic anthropologists quickly pointed out, however, that the kinds of rules proposed by formal pragmatics betrayed the linguists' assumption that the primary purpose of linguistic communication was to convey faithfully from speaker to hearer factual information about the world. This communication, moreover, was assumed to take place in a conversational setting between disinterested parties of equal social status. (Table 3.1 lists the components of formal linguistic analysis.)

Communication sometimes does involve the transmission of information between equals. Linguistic anthropologists were able to show, however, that such communication is only a small, and

TABLE 3.1 Components of Formal Linguistic Analysis

COMPONENT	APPLIES TO
Phonology	Phonemes/sound patterns
Morphology	Morphemes/word formation
Syntax	Sentence structure
Semantics	Meaning
Pragmatics	Language in use

highly idealized, part of what normally goes on when real people with differential linguistic and cultural knowledge, living in real societies characterized by social inequality, try to communicate with one another. As a result, linguistic anthropologists argue that every analysis of language use in cultural context must include information from ethnopragmatics. **Ethnopragmatics** is the study of the culturally and politically inflected rules of use that shape particular acts of speech communication among particular speakers and audiences, in the specific cultural settings in which they regularly occur. Put another way, the "universal" rules of formal pragmatics turn out to be so idealized and culture-bound that they are of little help when we try to understand what is going on in most verbal interactions in most cultural settings in most societies.

3.6 Language Contact and Change

Considering linguistic interaction within a context of struggle among speakers with unequal access to valued resources in a society has also refreshed our understanding of languages called pidgins and creoles. A **pidgin** language traditionally has been defined as a reduced language with a simplified grammar and vocabulary that develops when speakers of mutually unintelligible languages come into regular contact and so are forced to communicate with one another. Those who speak pidgins are native speakers of other, fully developed languages and use pidgins only in restricted settings with those who do not speak their native language; for this reason, pidgins are said to have no native speakers. However, when pidgins persist over two or more generations, they often begin to change. Specifically, their grammar sometimes becomes more complex, their vocabularies increase, they are used in a wider variety of social settings, and children learn them as first languages. When this happens, according to the traditional view, the pidgin has developed into a **creole** and functions just like any other natural human language.

For a long time, it was thought that the evolution from pidgin to creole was regular and inevitable, but it has become increasingly clear that pidgins and creoles can persist indefinitely along with other language varieties in the speech communities in which they are found. That is, speakers of pidgins also live in speech communities where different linguistic varieties have specialized uses. Moreover, such communities are regularly shaped by unequal power relations, which means that different varieties enjoy different levels of prestige and that those with more prestigious varieties in their verbal repertoires enjoy decided political and social advantages. Linguistic anthropologists and sociolinguists have pointed out that the most recent wave of pidginization followed European colonization throughout the world. They note further that pidgins and creoles developed under colonial (and postcolonial) political regimes in which mastery of the written language of the colonizer (e.g., English, French, or Dutch) has been a prerequisite for economic and social mobility. Thus, groups in the society that have been deprived of the opportunity to become literate in the colonizer's (or nation-state's) official "standard" language variety are also deprived of access to most of the wealth, power, and prestige in society.

Such a situation helps explain the sometimes violent struggles that occur in contemporary nation-states, especially in those that were once European colonies, about which language or languages will be the "official" language of schooling and of government. If people live in a society whose members speak a number of different languages and language varieties and if access to the most highly valued resources in society depends on fluency or literacy in only one official language, then it is easy to see that speakers of each language group will want their own language to be the official language.

Indeed, even when most members of a society are fluent or literate in the official language, they may be vigilant in policing the "purity" of that language, trying to eliminate linguistic borrowing from other languages. For example, when capitalist business practices and technology, originally developed in European languages, are imported into societies whose members do not speak a European language, the temptation is strong simply to borrow the European vocabulary and expressions for these practices and objects, rather than inventing new terms in the local language. The temptation is even stronger if printed instructional materials in the European language are also imported, for few poor countries on the periphery of the capitalist global economy have the resources to translate these materials into the languages of the local population. However, the influx of imported vocabulary may well be seen as a form of linguistic colonization. And like political colonization in the past, it is often resisted by **linguistic nationalism:** official, sometimes militant, efforts to proscribe the use of foreign terms and to promote the creation of alternatives in the local language.

Linguistic nationalism is hardly limited to former colonies of European powers. Citizens of European countries like France have periodically displayed linguistic nationalism when they protest the growing popularity among French speakers of expressions borrowed from American English. Like the citizens of former colonies, these French people fear that the influx of American English symbolizes a serious blow to the power and prestige of their own language and the nation to which its speakers belong.

3.7 Summary

In this chapter, we contrasted formal approaches to human language—phonetics, morphology, syntax, semantics, and pragmatics—with sociocultural perspectives that focus on language in use.

Both of these approaches had their origins in early anthropological interest in the variety of human languages.

For Further Reading

FORMAL LINGUISTICS

Akmajian et al. 2001

ANTHROPOLOGICAL LINGUISTICS

Agar 1994; Bonvillain 1993; Duranti 1997; Salzmann 1998

READINGS IN ANTHROPOLOGICAL LINGUISTICS

Blount 1995; Brenneis and Macaulay 1996

DISCOURSE

Hill and Irvine 1992; Schultz 1990

4

Culture
and the Individual

The key terms and concepts covered in this chapter, in the order in which they appear:

agency

cultural configurations

personality
culture-and-personality research
basic personality structure
modal personality
projective test

enculturation
child-rearing practices

ethnic psychoses

self
self-awareness
self-actualizing

independence training
dependence training

cognition

ethnoscience

schemas
prototypes

cognitive capacities
cognitive styles
global style
field-dependent
articulated style
field-independent

emotion

$\mathcal{S}$OME FIFTY YEARS AGO, American anthropologist Clyde Kluckhohn (1905–68) famously observed that, in some ways, every individual is like *all other* human beings, like *some other* human beings, and like *no other* human beings. Those attributes we share with *all* other human beings we share by virtue of being members of the same biological species, with the same anatomy, physiology, and range of physical and mental capacities, including the capacity for symbolic language and culture. Those attributes we share with *some* other human beings are *cultural* similarities. The great insight of social sciences like anthropology has been that individuals do *not* reinvent for themselves from scratch totally new cultural practices based on personal preference alone. Rather, we all begin by acquiring the shared ways of speaking, acting, and interpreting experience in use among the particular group of people among whom we grow up. At the same time, even human beings who have lived their entire lives immersed in the cultural practices of the same society are never simply cookie-cutter replicas of one another. Individual members of the same family or kinship group or ethnic group are very different from one another, based not only on such factors as gender and age differences but also on personal talents and inclination. Each of us has not only a unique set of genes (identical twins excepted!) but also a unique biography, making each of us, in some ways, like no other person on earth.

4.1 From Individualism to Agency

The Western capitalist societies that produced the first anthropologists were immersed in a culture that placed unusual emphasis on individuals. Unlike most other cultures from other places or times, capitalist culture exalts individuals and encourages (or forces) them to reject ties to other people, such as relatives, that they have not freely chosen. This position, called *individualism,* is based on a view of human nature that sees individuals as the primordial "natural" units in the human world. Individuals are believed to be endowed by nature with the desire to pursue their own personal self-interest above all else. While they might decide to sacrifice some of their natural, individual liberty to create societies in which the weak are protected from the strong, social obligations are always seen as "unnatural" restrictions on "natural" individual liberty. Seventeenth-century English philosopher Thomas Hobbes (1588–1679) imagined the life of early humans in a "state of nature" along these lines, an account that anthropologist Marshall Sahlins called the *origin myth of capitalism* (see Chapter 5 for a discussion of myth).

Individualism was well entrenched in the cultures to which the first social scientists belonged, but evidence from their reading and research caused many of them to question its universality. Within the bounds of a single society or cultural group, the differences between individuals are indeed striking. However, cross-cultural comparison immediately highlights all the attributes that those same individuals have in common, when contrasted with the members of another cultural group. Indeed, the value placed on individualism in the United States or Europe is recognized as a cultural matter as soon as capitalist culture is contrasted with noncapitalist cultures from elsewhere in the world (or even from earlier periods of European history). Therefore, social scientists in capitalist societies generally have been engaged in an ongoing debate concerning the degree to which the consciousness of individual human beings is or is not dominated by the beliefs and practices they acquire as members of particular societies.

Some anthropologists have used ethnographic evidence showing the ways individuals are molded by social, cultural, and historical forces in order to criticize extreme defenses of individualism used by Western elites to justify capitalist cultural practices. North American cultural anthropologists active early in the twentieth century, like Kluckhohn, seemed caught in the middle. Fully aware of the extent to which people's desires, values, and actions are molded by cultural forces, they nevertheless felt compelled to demonstrate the ways in which individuals might rise above cultural conditioning to assert their individuality. By the end of the twentieth century, anthropologists had mostly rejected the old-fashioned, extreme contrasts between "individual free will" and social, cultural, or historical "determinism." While they remain critical of defenses of individualism that ignore culture and history, they nevertheless now widely agree that individuals are not robots programmed by their cultures to think and behave only in prescribed ways. Contemporary anthropologists use the term **agency** to refer to individuals' abilities to reflect systematically on taken-for-granted cultural practices, to imagine alternatives, and to take independent action to pursue goals of their own choosing. Unlike deterministic accounts, this view recognizes degrees of individual freedom; but unlike discussions of "free will," it accepts that people's ideas are always embedded in the cultural practices of their own time and place, which restricts in some ways both the alternatives they are able to imagine and their abilities to act freely in pursuit of those alternatives.

4.2 Culture and Personality

How did anthropological ideas about the relationship between culture and the individual develop? In North America, the earliest efforts arose as Boasian anthropologists sought a persuasive way to characterize differences between cultures. A key move was made by Ruth Benedict (1887–1948) who, in her 1934 book *Patterns of Culture*, urged her readers to think of the integrated patterns of a particular culture, or **cultural configurations,** as if they were the integrated patterns of an individual personality. This metaphor—that cultures were essentially individual personalities "writ large"—was perhaps an inevitable development in a society that exalted individualism. Indeed, Boas and his students were persuaded that psychology—the study of individual minds—held important clues for the understanding of culture.

As a result, cultural anthropologists began to look at individual personality for evidence that would reveal the unique configurations of the culture to which an individual belonged. In general, **personality** refers to ways of thinking, feeling, and acting that are unique to a specific individual and that might explain that individual's consistency of behavior over time and across a variety of social settings. Anthropologists who offered hypotheses about the factors responsible for the development, structure, and function of individual personalities shared a number of concerns with psychologists. But whereas psychologists typically studied these matters only among members of their own society, anthropologists explicitly used cross-cultural ethnographic information to assess the degree to which distinct personality configurations were regularly associated with particular cultures. In the middle decades of the twentieth century, this became known as **culture-and-personality research.**

Anthropologists of the culture-and-personality school have investigated a range of issues concerning the relationship between individuals and culture. For example, if a culture could be understood as an individual personality writ large, did this mean that the individual personalities of all those who belonged to the culture were the same? One psychological anthropologist, Abraham Kardiner, proposed that all members of a society did come to acquire what he called a **basic personality structure** in the course of individual development, as they adapted to what he called the *primary institutions* of their society. Primary institutions include established ways that members of the society organize family life (including child care and sexual expression) and economic life (how they make a living). Basic personality structures would be similar throughout a society if all members had to adapt to the same primary institutions. Kardiner also spoke, however, of *secondary institutions:* established religious or ritual practices that help individuals cope with the challenges presented by primary institutions—for example, when subsistence horticulturalists develop elaborate rainmaking rituals, which they observe every planting season, to reduce their anxieties about the disaster that would ensue if the rains failed and their crops died. Basic personality structure would change, Kardiner argued, if a people's primary institutions changed. And he predicted that larger societies with a more complex division of labor would generate a wider range of personality types than would smaller societies with more homogenous institutions.

Many critics of culture-and-personality research found even these specifications to be vague and difficult to demonstrate. Later studies attempted to gather a much richer body of data on personality traits from a wide range of sources and to use statistical analysis to interpret the results. Such studies preferred to speak not of basic personality but of **modal personality,** a "typical" personality for members of a particular society, which was revealed as the central tendency of a frequency distribution.

Debates about basic versus modal personalities highlight one of the persistent challenges of culture-and-personality research: how to gather valid information about personality characteristics. One way anthropologists tried to meet this challenge involves supplementing the usual range of anthropological fieldwork techniques with testing methods borrowed from psychology.

One technique that has been widely used in culture-and-personality research is the **projective test.** For example, the anthropologist may present informants with a series of ambiguous images or sketchy drawings and ask them to describe what they think the images or drawings represent. Because the images and drawings are deliberately vague and open to a wide variety of possible interpretations, anthropologists assume that subjects will *project* their own personalities into the images; that is, they will interpret the images in a way that reveals their own personality traits and psychological preoccupations. If culture truly is a prime shaper of individual personality, then subjects from the same culture should produce very similar results on the same projective test. Unfortunately, experience has shown that responses to projective tests, like the images used in the tests, are not always easy to interpret. Making sense of them requires considerable additional information about the culture of the subjects and about the subjects themselves, including their understanding of the purpose of the test-taking situation.

4.3 Enculturation

Some anthropologists doing culture-and-personality research have asked questions about how individual personalities develop as children mature into adults. Unlike most conventional psychologists, however, anthropologists do not automatically assume that personality development is identical in all human societies. For example, Margaret Mead, another student of Boas, explicitly addressed this issue in her first important book, *Coming of Age in Samoa,* published in 1928. Mead's work in Samoa focused on **enculturation:** the social processes through which children come to adopt the ways of thinking, feeling, and behaving considered appropriate for adults in their culture. Mead argued that the stressful period of adolescence experienced by maturing children in Western industrial societies was neither universal nor inevitable. She used ethnographic data to show that children growing up in Samoan culture developed a different set of personality traits and experienced little or no adolescent stress.

A generation of cultural anthropologists in North America followed Mead's example, carrying out research on enculturation processes in a wide range of different societies. Their work was given a strengthened theoretical framework when some anthropologists, including Mead herself, began to consider the ideas of Sigmund Freud (1856–1939). Freud offered a framework of psychological stages of development (somewhat different for males and for females) through which every child supposedly passed on the way to adulthood. He further argued that children's success or failure in passing through these stages would determine their degree of mental health in adulthood, explaining a variety of adult psychological disturbances in terms of an individual's lack of success at one or another stage. The resulting psychological damage ranged from fairly mild *neuroses* to extremely serious *psychoses,* which were so debilitating that individuals appeared to lose touch with reality and were unable to establish satisfying lives with others in society.

Freud's emphasis on the importance of individual experience in early childhood for the formation of adult personality suggested new ways to conceptualize enculturation. Anthropologists who adopted a Freudian orientation focused, as he did, on the shaping of children's emotional development as they negotiated relationships with their parents in the first three years of life. But they also tested the claims of Freudian psychology against ethnographic evidence in a wide range of cultures. After all, Freud's theories were based on his experiences with late-nineteenth-century middle-class Viennese patients with psychological disturbances of one kind or another. Anthropologists wanted to determine how much of Freudian psychology was culture-bound and how much might be universally valid in all human societies.

Because Freud stressed the importance of young children's experiences in their families, psychological anthropologists began to pay attention to **child-rearing practices:** the ways in which adults (especially parents) in a particular culture tried to shape children's behavior to bring it in line with culture-specific ideals of appropriateness. They would study, for example, the way in which infants were handled: Were they allowed to move their arms and legs freely, or were they tightly swaddled for several months? Could such treatment be shown to have consequences for the child's later personality development? Like Freud, these psychological anthropologists focused on key events such as the weaning of nursing babies from the breast or the teaching of bowel and bladder control (i.e., toilet training). Freud considered emotionally fraught power struggles in these areas to be inevitable and frequently traumatic for children. Thus, anthropologists were interested in what the personality consequences for children might be in cultures that, for example, allowed children to nurse until 3 or 4 years of age or in which indoor toilets and Western sanitation practices were absent.

Cross-cultural child-rearing studies produced a wealth of information about the different ways in which children were enculturated to become successful adults in different cultures. This information convinced many anthropologists that Freud's ideas were indeed heavily influenced by the middle-class, patriarchal, Viennese culture in which they had been formed. Many anthropologists concluded that the repressive values and practices of that culture (particularly its restrictions on females) did more to explain the neuroses and psychoses Freud identified than did his supposedly universal series of developmental stages. Not only were such maladjustments absent in cultures with different values and practices, but sometimes the "maladjusted" behavior was viewed positively. For example, individuals who would be labeled psychotic by a Freudian because they claimed to hear the voices of invisible beings or to converse with the dead have been given high status in many societies as *shamans,* a particular kind of religious practitioner and curer (see Chapter 5 for details on shamans). In addition, ethnographers have encountered forms of beliefs and behavior in many non-Western societies that are considered "abnormal" by members of those societies but are found in no other societies and often do not appear on the diagnostic lists of medically recognized psychological disorders that have been developed by Western psychology and psychiatry. These culture-bound syndromes have been called **ethnic psychoses:** mental and emotional behaviors and experiences that are viewed as unusual and disturbing to the members of particular ethnic groups. Examples include such disorders as the so-called arctic hysterias recognized by a number of peoples living in circumpolar latitudes and anorexia nervosa, the eating disorder restricted to Western industrial societies in which individuals (mostly young women) believe they are too fat, refuse to eat, and sometimes die as a result.

Among other things, this focus on child-rearing practices promised to shed light on larger cultural issues related to the particular role accorded individualism in Western capitalist societies. The prototype of successful individuals in these societies is the *entrepreneur;* those individuals who are particularly adept in finding ways to pursue their own individual self-interest. Such entrepreneurs are admired for their ability to break with tradition, especially when they generate new ideas and new wealth by means of capitalist business practices. Many people, both in Western societies and elsewhere, believed that all societies that wanted to prosper and become "modern" would have to produce similar kinds of individuals, but such personality types were far more common in the West. Anthropologists and others wondered if there was something about the way children were enculturated in the United States and Europe that imparted to them the skills and motivation to become entrepreneurs.

4.4 The Self

Strong individualists, for example, seemed to regard themselves as distinct and unique objects, separate from other things and individuals in their society. This has been called a person's sense of

self. Successful individualists, however, also possess a high degree of **self-awareness.** That is, they can realistically assess their likes, dislikes, strengths, and weaknesses, as well as the degree to which their goals do or do not mesh with those of other people and institutions. They are able and willing to pursue personal goals that correspond to their unique talents and opportunities, even in the face of social opposition. To use the expression popularized by Abraham Kardiner, a key figure in culture-and-personality research around the years of World War II, such individuals are **self-actualizing.** For many observers, self-actualizing individuals, each seeking to develop as fully as possible a unique set of gifts in pursuit of unique personal goals, had made Western nations rich and powerful. Did Western child-rearing practices hold the key?

Comparative work by a number of anthropologists suggested that, indeed, the way children were reared affected their willingness and ability to self-actualize. Anthropologists came to distinguish two broad kinds of child-rearing practices. One kind, sometimes called **independence training,** engages adults with children in ways that promote the children's ability to rely on themselves, rather than others, to achieve personal goals. Such training is the rule in middle-class North American households, for example. These parents encourage babies to sleep alone in their own beds, in their own rooms; they reward young children for accomplishing simple tasks without assistance; they expect older children to perform household chores alone; and they may encourage teenagers to earn the money for fashionable clothes, a car, or college expenses. By the time they reach adulthood, these children will have the expectation that their future well-being is in their own hands and that nobody else, often including their parents, can or should help them define or achieve their goals. They are, in other words, primed to self-actualize, possessing all the basic skills and experiences needed by a capitalist entrepreneur.

Most societies of the world, however, do not traditionally rear their children to become independent and self-reliant; quite the contrary, their enculturation practices have been described as a form of **dependence training.** Most societies, in most times and places, have very strong group structures—kinship groups, religious or ethnic groups, regional groups, classes, or castes. Culture in these societies regularly teaches that each group member's first duty is to act in such a way as to promote the well-being of the group, because only if the group is strong will the individual be strong. Children are not encouraged to strike out on their own but instead are encouraged to conform to adults' wishes and to rely on them to protect their interests. Regardless of personal inclinations, for example, children would be likely to allow elders to arrange their marriages, having come to accept, however grudgingly, that their individual welfare cannot be separated from the welfare of the group and that group leaders know best.

Although culture-and-personality research brought to light much important cross-cultural evidence, it was increasingly criticized for drawing sweeping conclusions on the basis of equivocal or incomplete evidence. To the extent that these researchers relied on Freudian psychology to justify their claims, their conclusions were questioned when Freud's ideas eventually came under fire. Feminists, for example, argued that his theories were so deeply rooted in Western European patriarchal biases that they could offer little insight. Other works by non-Western scholars and clinicians raised similar criticisms, based on the difficulties they encountered in applying Freud's work to their own societies. In addition, a revolution in psychology, which focused on the psychological roots of rational thinking, came to supplant the Freudian models of human emotional development. A key figure in this transformation was the Swiss psychologist Jean Piaget (1896–1980), who offered his own developmental scheme. Piaget described four stages in the development of rational thinking in children, from their earliest explorations of the world around them to mastery of the highest levels of abstract calculation in higher mathematics.

4.5 Cognition and Cognitive Anthropology

Anthropologists inspired by Piaget abandoned the culture-and-personality orientation of their predecessors and began to emphasize cross-cultural studies of **cognition:** the mental processes by means of which individual human beings make sense of and incorporate information about the world. Rather than focusing on individual emotional and sexual development in the context of family relationships, cognitive anthropologists were interested in the effect culture might have on perception, reason, logic, and the way people classified objects and experiences in the world. This change in orientation first became well known in the work of anthropologists in the 1950s and 1960s who came to be known as ethnoscientists (see Chapter 3). **Ethnoscience** as a school of thought was interested in the ways people in different cultures categorized their experiences and classified objects and events in the wider world. Working in the native language of their informants, they made great efforts to expunge the influence of their own Western scientific (or etic) categories and to faithfully elicit their informants' indigenous (or emic) systems of classification (see Chapter 3 for further details). Cognitive anthropologists who studied non-Western classification systems discovered that, although there was considerable overlap between, for example, indigenous classifications of plants and animals and biological classifications offered by Western scientists, usually there were also significant differences. Often, these differences had to do with the functional or symbolic significance of certain plants or animals or other objects found in everyday life. Objects or events might be classified as "the same," for example, because they were all associated with the same daily activity or jointly figured in a key ritual.

These segments of culturally significant activity were understood as key cognitive units, or **schemas,** whose overall configuration overshadowed the parts of which they were composed. This meant that objects or events took their central meanings from the role they played in schemas of high cultural salience, not because they all possessed the same set of abstract attributes. Put another way, people classify objects in terms of **prototypes:** typical instances of objects or events they are familiar with and know most about. English speakers living in the temperate United States, for example, are likely to think of robins as prototypical birds because of their high level of experiential and cultural significance; that is, we associate robins with the return of spring and renewed natural growth. Other living things will then be classified as "birds" based on the degree to which they resemble robins; for example, small songbirds like cardinals will be much closer to the bird prototype than will large flightless birds like ostriches.

Prototypes and schemas clearly are related to each other. Together, they provide groups of people with distinctive, shared cognitive tools they can use to make sense not only of the regularities of everyday life but also of new, unexpected objects or experiences that challenge those regularities. Some cognitive anthropologists have specialized in schema theory, which focuses on the ways in which preexisting cultural schemas and prototypes shape expectations, encouraging us to interpret new experiences in ways that conform to past experience and even to reconfigure our memories of past experiences to bring them into line with present understandings.

Some of the questions asked by cognitive anthropologists parallel the questions asked by culture-and-personality theorists: Do different cultures shape individuals with different kinds of cognitive skills? Are the cognitive skills required for success in the world of Western capitalism themselves products of capitalist culture? Anthropologists generally agree that all members of the human species share the same general range of **cognitive capacities:** innate abilities to classify, compare, draw inferences, and so forth. If adults in different cultures perform differently when asked to complete the same cognitive tasks, therefore, does this mean that their culture has somehow molded their cognitive capacities in a particular direction? Cognitive anthropologists carried out cross-cultural tests designed to provide answers. Many used tests borrowed from psychologists, such as cards showing objects of different shapes and colors, which research subjects were then asked to classify and reclassify as many times as they could.

As with projective tests used by culture-and-personality researchers, the results of the tests used by cognitive anthropologists often were ambiguous and difficult to interpret, and for many of the same reasons. Specifically, it was not always clear that the subjects understood the purpose of the test the way the

TABLE 4.1   Cognitive Styles

GLOBAL	ARTICULATED
Field-Dependent	*Field-Independent*
Attention to wider context first; then focus on internal elements	Attention to individual elements first; then focus on wider context

anthropologists did, and subjects frequently drew upon local cultural understandings of which the researchers were initially unaware, in order to make sense of the test.

4.6 Cognitive Styles

Nevertheless, this research did yield interesting information concerning what have been called **cognitive styles:** typical ways that individuals (or members of the same group) tackle a particular task. Anthropologists were struck by the fact that many non-Western subjects who had never been to a Western-type school typically used what was called a **global style;** that is, they first focused their attention on the situation as a whole, before paying attention to the detailed elements that made it up. Global style was said to be **field-dependent;** that is, subjects required knowledge of the broader context in which the elements were embedded in order to make sense of the elements themselves. This contrasted with the **articulated style** regularly used by educated Western subjects. In this style, they first paid attention to the detailed elements that make up the situation and only later looked for the relationships these elements might have with one another. Articulated style was said to be **field-independent;** that is, subjects could consider individual elements in themselves, without paying attention to the context in which they were embedded. (Table 4.1 summarizes the key features of cognitive styles.)

The field-independent, articulated style that required people to ignore context looked as though it might be the outcome of independence training, in which self-actualizing individuals are taught to ignore contextual relationships that might restrict them. Similarly, the field-dependent global style looked as though it might be the result of dependence training, in which individuals are urged to embed or submerge their personal identity into the wider contextual identity of the group. In fact, as cognitive anthropologists did more detailed work in both Western and non-Western cultures, they showed that *all* people in *all* cultures are able to make use of global and articulated styles; the main differences have to do with which cognitive styles are considered appropriate for which tasks. Because both rules of appropriateness and kinds of tasks vary considerably from culture to culture, there is a high likelihood that people from different cultures will interpret the "same" task in different ways and will choose different cognitive strategies to cope with it. However, one big difference does seem to hold universally: those individuals, regardless of cultural background, who have experienced Western-style schooling consistently perform like educated people from Western cultures on cognitive tests.

4.7 Emotion

In recent years, some cognitive anthropologists have returned to a study of **emotion,** but their emphasis is quite different from that of the culture-and-personality theorists. Rather than emphasizing emotion as rooted in the body or sexuality, cognitive anthropologists view emotions as categories of feeling or patterns of affect. These anthropologists build on work by social psychologists who have argued that what English speakers call "emotion" actually combines a fairly undifferentiated physical arousal with specific meanings that give the arousal its particular "emotional" quality. Anthropologists focus on the meanings used to distinguish emotional experiences, arguing that different cultures create distinct categories of feeling associated with specific cultural meanings. One consequence of this approach is the conclusion that "emotions" are not "the same" everywhere but are heavily influenced by local cultural categories of feeling. Indeed, some anthropologists argue that without culturally created categories of feeling to help them, people do not know what they feel! That is, people's emotional experiences are often ambiguous, and anthropologists study how cultural beliefs about feeling help resolve such ambiguities by specifying which kinds of persons are entitled to feel which kinds of culturally specific emotions in which culturally defined contexts.

4.8 Summary

In this chapter, we considered a variety of ways in which anthropologists have studied the degree to which culture provides a context within which individuals are shaped. We looked at how, over the years, anthropologists have changed their approaches to the issues of cognition, perception, and emotion and how the field has gone from a self-definition of culture and personality to cognitive anthropology.

For Further Reading

GENERAL OVERVIEWS

Bock 1994

CULTURE AND PERSONALITY APPROACHES

Barnouw 1985

CROSS-CULTURAL PSYCHOANALYTIC APPROACHES

Doi 1985; Kakar 1981

CULTURE AND COGNITION

Cole and Scribner 1974; Lave 1988

PSYCHOLOGICAL ANTHROPOLOGY APPROACHES

Ingham 1996; Schwartz, White, and Lutz 1992

CULTURE AND EMOTION

Lutz 1988

5
Religion and Worldview

The key terms and concepts covered in this chapter, in the order in which they appear:

worldview

religion
animism
ancestor cult
gods
polytheistic religions
mana
oracle
dogma
orthodoxy

myths
origin myths
ritual
religious rituals
prayer

sacrifice
congregation
orthopraxy
rite of passage
liminal period
communitas
magic

witchcraft

shamans
priests

conversion
syncretism
revitalization

Human beings in all cultures try to make sense of their experience in ways that link them meaningfully to the wider world. Anthropologists use the term **worldview** to refer to the result of such interpretive efforts: an encompassing picture of reality based on a set of shared assumptions about how the world works. Anthropologists have long been interested in how worldviews are constructed and how people use them to make sense of their experiences. Worldviews establish symbolic frameworks that highlight certain significant domains of social experience while downplaying others. Multiple worldviews may coexist in a single society, or a single worldview may dominate.

5.1 Religion

As they began to compare cultures, anthropologists repeatedly encountered worldviews that reminded them of the religions they knew from Euro-American societies. Over the years, they have tried with mixed success to craft definitions of religion that took these diverse beliefs and practices into account. Most definitions that are currently in use do seem to agree that a **religion** is a worldview in which people personify cosmic forces and devise ways to deal with them that resemble the ways they deal with powerful human beings in their society. In practice, this means that people with religious worldviews conceive of the universe as populated by powerful forces that may understand human language and take an active interest in human affairs. Although their presence ordinarily may not be detectable by the human senses, they are never very far away. They may monitor human behavior and send punishments to those who violate moral rules, but if human beings approach them in the proper manner, they may use their power to confer benefits. Such personified beings have been variously called gods, goddesses, spirits, ancestors, ghosts, or souls.

While some anthropologists continue to use the term *supernatural* to refer to such beings or the realm they inhabit, most contemporary anthropological writing on religion avoids this term because it imposes on other societies a distinction between "natural" and "supernatural" worlds that those societies often do not recognize. Similar problems affect many other terms that Western observers, anthropologists included, have used to describe and analyze different religions. For this reason, some influential definitions of religion do not mention beings of any kind but focus on symbols and the ways in which people use symbols to bring meaning and coherence to the interpretation of their experiences.

Anthropologists have suggested a variety of reasons why religion seems to be so important in human societies: it is a way for people to deal with uncertainty that they cannot otherwise control, it is a way to provide meaning for people's lives, it explains the otherwise unexplainable (suffering, death, the mysterious in everyday life), and it helps to create social solidarity among those who adhere to it.

Confronted with enormous diversity in the religious traditions of the world, anthropologists proceeded to classify them according to type. For example, some religions propose that objects like trees or stones or rivers may have souls or spirits associated with them who may interact with people for good or for ill. The nineteenth-century English anthropologist E. B. Tylor (1832–1917) used the term **animism** to describe religions based on belief in the existence of such souls or spirit beings (*anima* is the Latin word for "soul"). Although most contemporary anthropologists no longer use this term because of the disparaging connotations it has acquired over the years, it may still be found in discussions in the field of comparative religion in which "world religions" like Christianity or Islam are contrasted with "animist religions" in which the only personified forces that are recognized are souls or spirits associated with features of the local landscape. The set of beliefs and practices associated with these souls and spirits are certainly real in some societies in the world today—traditional Inuit and Australian Aboriginal societies, for example—but many scholars prefer to use terms like "traditional religion" to avoid the persisting implication that animism is something that "more advanced" societies have evolved away from.

In societies where the connections of kinship do not end with physical death, religion may take the form of what is called an **ancestor cult** (for more about kinship see Chapter 9). In these systems, the ancestors are believed to maintain a strong interest in the lives of their descendents and are believed to act to maintain social order by sending sickness or other misfortune when the rules by which people are supposed to live are violated. In these societies, it is often the most senior people who gain great power from the ancestor cult, since they are closest to becoming ancestors.

Other societies recognize the existence of sentient and personified forces that are less local and more powerful. The entities may be called **gods,** and traditions in which there are many such beings are sometimes called **polytheistic religions.** The gods in polytheistic religions may have many of the personal attributes of human beings, including gender, and they may produce children with one another or with human beings, as did the gods in the religion of ancient Greece. But in some societies, the cosmic force or forces recognized are barely personalized at all. This is true in the case of **mana,** a Melanesian term introduced into anthropology in the nineteenth century to designate a cosmic force whose only human-like attribute is the ability to respond to human beings who use the correct symbolic formulas when they want to harness or channel this force for their own purposes. Another minimally personified cosmic force is an **oracle,** an invisible force capable of understanding questions addressed to it in human language and willing to respond truthfully using symbolic means that human beings with the proper cultural knowledge can interpret.

The beliefs people have regarding the nature of the world and the beings that inhabit it form one part of a religious worldview. But societies differ in how systematically they have organized this knowledge and in how much leeway they allow their members to offer alternative interpretations. In some societies, religious knowledge of this kind is highly detailed, carefully organized, and formally passed on from generation to generation. When the truths it is believed to contain may not be questioned, such knowledge is sometimes called **dogma** or **orthodoxy** (correct belief). In other societies, however, religious beliefs are not systematized, and no great emphasis is placed on orthodoxy, with the result that different adherents to the tradition may offer varied or conflicting interpretations of it.

5.2 Myth

Important components of religious traditions are **myths**: stories whose truth seems self-evident because they do such a good job of integrating personal experiences with a wider set of assumptions about the way society, or the world in general, must operate. Those myths that explain the creation of the world or of particular features of the landscape or of human beings are often called **origin myths.** Other myths may recount the adventures of the gods, the consequences of their interactions with human beings, or what will happen when the world ends. Although enduring religious myths are believed to embody important insights into life's purposes, they are more than morality tales. They are usually a highly developed verbal art form as well, recited for purposes of both entertainment and instruction, and the occasion of their telling offers verbal artists the opportunity to demonstrate their creative, aesthetic skills. Frequently, the "official" myth tellers are the most powerful or respected groups in society, such as the elders or political leaders or religious specialists. Myths have a social importance because, if they are taken literally, they tell people where they have come from and where they are going and, therefore, how they should live right now.

The study of myth has always been important in anthropology. Over time, two major approaches to the study of myth have had a lasting impact on the field. The first approach comes from Bronislaw Malinowski, who argued that myths are charters for social action; that is, the beings and places who figure in the myths can be referred to by living people in order to justify present-day social arrangements. For example, an origin myth about a particular kinship group may describe where members of the group first appeared on the land and the places they subsequently visited. This myth can be used by living members of that kinship group to defend their claims to land in the territories that their ancestors visited and to negate claims to the same land made by other members of the society. In short, to understand why myths have the content they do and how that content changes over time, one must understand the social beliefs and practices of the people who tell them.

The second approach to myth comes from the French anthropologist Claude Lévi-Strauss (1908–). While not denying Malinowski's observations about the practical uses to which myths could be put, Lévi-Strauss showed that the very structures of mythic narratives are meaningful and worth studying in their own right. In this sense, myths are cognitive tools for resolving logical contradictions in human social experience that cannot otherwise be overcome in the world that human beings know. In particular, myths are attempts to deal with oppositions of continuing concern to members of a particular society, such as the opposition between men and women, nature and culture, or life and death, or opposing styles of postmarital residence (postmarital residence is discussed in Chapter 10). Although these oppositions may be irresolvable in everyday life, myths offer an imaginative realm in which alternative possibilities and their (frequently undesirable) consequences can be explored.

Many scholars, including Malinowski and Lévi-Strauss, have assumed that the people who believe in myths typically are unaware how their myths are structured or how they use myths to defend their interests. Recent anthropological work, however, acknowledges that ordinary members of a society often *are* aware of how their myths structure meaning. And it is precisely this awareness that permits them to manipulate the way myths are told or interpreted in order to gain support for the version or interpretation that furthers their goals.

5.3 Ritual

Anthropologists use the term **ritual** to identify certain repetitive social practices, many of which have nothing to do with religion. A ritual is composed of a sequence of symbolic activities, set off from the social routines of everyday life, recognizable by members of the society as a ritual, and closely connected to a specific set of ideas that are often encoded in myth. What gives rituals their power is that participants assert that the authorization for the ritual comes from outside themselves—from the state, society, God, the ancestors, or "tradition." For example, in a courtroom, when people rise as the judge enters or refer to the judge as "your honor," they are not doing so because they feel like it or because the individual judge insists on it but because of the authority of the state and the Constitution. Thus, by responding in court, "Not guilty, your honor," one is accepting the authority of not just the judge but also of the court, the justice system, and the Constitution. (Indeed, this is the difference between a wedding rehearsal and a wedding.) Even when rituals are invented or transformed, those involved with them attempt to connect the innovations to external sources of authority. For example, at our university's graduation ceremony, the graduates are asked to applaud the parents, relatives, and friends who have helped them achieve that moment. While this part of the ritual was proposed by a former president, his justification for the innovation was that it took account of something profoundly important in the social world that the institution needed to acknowledge, and it was in keeping with the other elements of the graduation ceremony.

Much work in recent years in anthropology has explored the relationship between ritual and power, and much of this work has concentrated on rituals that are not religious. But the role of ritual in religious contexts remains an important area of study. If the universe is indeed populated by powerful personified beings that take an interest in human affairs, then it is to the very great benefit of human beings to devise ways of dealing with them. All religious worldviews assume that communication between personified cosmic forces is possible and potentially beneficial, but it can take place only if carried out in the correct way. Most religious traditions have developed specialized social routines for communication with the gods that, if performed correctly, should ensure successful communication. As a consequence, **religious rituals** are distinctive in that they regularly involve attempts to influence or gain the sympathy of a particular personified cosmic being. One

Sacrifice → offering up something

kind of religious ritual involves addressing these personified forces in human speech, often out loud, while holding the body in a conventional posture of respect; this is called **prayer.** Another kind of religious ritual involves offering something of value (goods, services, money, or an appropriately slaughtered animal) to the invisible forces or their agents; this is called **sacrifice.** Prayer and sacrifice frequently are performed when members of a religious tradition come together in processions, meetings, or convocations; this is called **congregation.** Coming together of people

Members of some religious traditions insist that correct ritual behavior is essential at times of prayer or sacrifice and that any deviation will nullify the ritual. Indeed, some religious traditions aim to ritualize virtually every waking act adherents perform, a style of religious practice called **orthopraxy** (correct practice). Not all religious traditions that value ritual are orthoprax, however; many entertain a range of opinion regarding correct practice, and individual people or independent religious practitioners are free to develop their own rituals or variants of more broadly recognized rituals. *Orthopraxy → correct practice

One particular kind of ritual has drawn considerable attention from anthropologists: the **rite of passage,** which occurs when one or more members of a society are ritually transformed from one kind of social person into another. Rites of passage often are initiations into adulthood, when girls are made women or boys made men, but they may also mark marriages (when single people become a married couple), the birth of children (when a new life enters the world), or funerals (when living kin become ancestors). These and other so-called life-cycle transitions frequently are marked by rituals that connect participants to ancestors or gods or other cosmic forces. Anthropologists point out that rites of passage regularly follow a three-part sequence. First, the ritual passengers (i.e., the persons who are changing their social position) are *separated* from their previous, everyday existence. Next, they pass through a *transitional* state, in which they are neither in the old position nor yet in the new one. Finally, with their new status, they are *reaggregated,* or brought back, into the everyday social world. The second, transitional stage of the ritual was particularly

Handwritten margin and interlinear notes:

(c) prayer way to connect speech

(s) correct ritual behavior is essential

some can devert

rite of passage

3 steps

① seperated ② transitional (limited period)

③ reaggregated (brought back)

*

2nd state

significant for anthropologist Victor Turner (1920–83), who referred to it as the **liminal period** (from the Latin word *limen,* meaning "threshold"). Turner noted that when people are on the threshold, they are "betwixt and between," neither in nor out. In rites of passage, the symbolism associated with the transitional period often expresses that ambiguity: it is described as being in the womb, being invisible, being in the wilderness, or as death. Ritual passengers in the liminal stage tend to develop an intense comradeship with one another; social distinctions that separated them before the ritual and will separate them again afterward become irrelevant. Turner called this liminal social relationship **communitas,** which is best understood as an unstructured or minimally structured community of equal individuals. In rites of passage concerned with initiation, for example, the liminal period is a time in which those being initiated are tutored in knowledge and skills that their elders believe they must master if they are to be successful in the stage of life they are about to enter.

learning period of time

→ * Communitas → liminal social relationship/unstructured community of equal individuals.

5.4 Magic and Witchcraft

Anthropologists have also paid much attention to another form of ritual called **magic.** The persistence of definitions of magic that include the term *supernatural* is another indication of the difficulty of using one culture's definitions to describe practices in other cultures. Generally, magic refers to ritual practices that do not have technically or scientifically apparent effects but are believed by the actors to have an influence on the outcome of practical matters. People may believe that the correct performance of such rituals can result in healing, the growth of plants, the recovery of lost or stolen objects, getting a hit in baseball, or safely sailing an outrigger canoe in the Pacific Ocean. The classic anthropological explanation of magic comes from the research of Bronislaw Malinowski in the Trobriand Islands early in the twentieth century. Malinowski suggested that all living societies have developed effective knowledge and practical techniques for dealing with the world. At the same time, however, they also realize that their practical control over the world has limits. Where their

M def. of magic

"We" can only control so much   — limitations

techniques and knowledge are sufficient for accomplishing their goals, magic is not used. But when the outcome is uncertain, regardless of the skill and insight people may have, they are likely to resort to magical practices. The use of magic in such situations, Malinowski argued, has the practical function of reducing anxiety, thereby allowing people to concentrate on what they are able to control. He observed, for example, that Trobriand Islanders he knew used outrigger canoes to go fishing both in the protected lagoons around the islands and also in the Pacific Ocean. When they fished in the lagoons, which were safe and secure, they put their canoes into the water and got straight to work. But when they were going past the lagoons into the open ocean, which was unpredictable and dangerous, they recited spells and used other techniques throughout the voyage.

Traditional anthropological discussions of magic have emphasized that most magical practices seem to be based on one of two underlying ideas: like affects like, and things that at one time have been in contact continue to affect each other even when they are separated. Practices based on the idea that like affects like have been called *imitative magic*. A familiar example is the so-called voodoo doll: a pin stuck in the back of the doll will supposedly cause a stabbing pain in the back of the victim the doll represents. Today, anthropologists suggest that *analogy* is a more accurate description of the underlying principle behind such a practice than is *imitation*. This is because the symbolic relations between the ritual objects (i.e., the doll and the pin) and their magical "world" is extended, by analogy, to the target of the magic (i.e., the enemy) and its "world." In other words, the ritual sticking of a pin into the back of a doll is analogous to the sticking of a (magical) knife into the back of a human enemy. The causal connections believed to operate in the world of the ritual objects (dolls, pins, herbs, etc.) and the invisible forces that link the two worlds together are the result of particular cultural understandings not shared by all human observers.

Ritual practices based on the idea that things that have once been in contact continue to affect each other even when they are separated have been called *contagious magic*. For example, hair or nail clippings were once part of a person's body, and a personal garment has had sustained contact with the body of the person who wears it. Many societies have the belief that if one can secure a few strands of hair or nail clippings from an individual, or a piece of clothing that the person has worn, and work a spell over these things, the spell will affect that person. Because wholes always remain connected to their parts, even when the parts are no longer in contact with the whole, acting on the part (e.g., the shirt) will continue to affect the whole (i.e., the person who wore it).

In the late nineteenth century, when unilineal evolutionary schemes were popular in anthropology (see Chapter 12 for details), many anthropologists proposed that magic and religion were separate stages in the progressive evolution of human thought that culminated in science. But subsequent ethnographic research, especially work done in the past few decades, has made it clear that magic, religion, and science may coexist in the same society and may even be used by the same people, who resort to different ways of coping with the world in different social contexts. In some cases, people in search of a solution to a serious problem, such as infertility, may be unwilling to dismiss any beliefs or practices that offer a solution, alternatively consulting medical doctors, praying in church, and consulting practitioners of alternative therapies that some might argue are based on magic.

It is important to stress that interest in identifying and defining the true nature of magic was historically of greatest concern to two categories of Western critics: missionaries eager to demonstrate the superiority of their version of "religion" over what they considered to be the superstitious "magical" practices of "primitive peoples," and defenders of science, who wanted to demonstrate its superiority over both magic and religion. The more science was stressed as the embodiment of rationality, the more necessary it became to stress the "irrational" features of religion and magic.

Anthropologists committed to cultural relativism in the early twentieth century were more interested in stressing the sensible side of seemingly exotic beliefs and practices like magic and witchcraft. Malinowski, as we have seen, focused on the positive practical side effects of belief in the efficacy of magic spells. E. E. Evans-Pritchard (1902–73), in his classic monograph *Witchcraft, Oracles, and Magic among the Azande* (first published in 1937), demonstrated that the beliefs and practices associated with all three phenomena were perfectly logical, if one accepted certain basic assumptions about the world.

Among the Azande, **witchcraft** involves the performance of evil by human beings believed to possess an innate, nonhuman "witchcraft substance" that can be activated without the individual's awareness. (Other anthropologists, using Azande witchcraft as their prototype, have applied the term to similar beliefs and practices found in other societies.) For the Azande, witchcraft tends to explain misfortune when other possibilities have been discounted. For example, if a good potter carefully prepares his pots and fires them as he always does, but they still break, he will attribute his misfortune to witchcraft, and his neighbors will probably believe him. But if a careless potter is sloppy when firing his pots, and they break, he may claim that witchcraft was the cause, but no one who knows him will believe it.

Evans-Pritchard showed that the entire system of Azande beliefs and practices concerning witchcraft, oracles, and magic was perfectly rational if one assumed that unseen forces exist in the world and that nothing happens to people by accident. For example, when someone falls very ill or dies, the Azande assume that the person has been bewitched. But the Azande are not helpless, because they know they can consult oracles who will help them pinpoint the witch responsible. Once the oracle has identified the witch, they can send a ritual message to the accused witch, who can offer a ritual reply that will stop the witchcraft, if indeed he (it is usually a man) has been the cause of it. If the bewitched person dies, however, the next step is to obtain vengeance magic, which can be used to seek out the witch responsible and kill him.

The Azande do not collapse in fear in the presence of witchcraft because they know how to deal with it. Moreover, they make an accusation of witchcraft only after cross-checking the oracle's pronouncements carefully. Because all the steps in the process are carried out in great secrecy, who has accused whom and who has killed whom with vengeance magic is not open to public scrutiny, so that contradictions in the system are rarely exposed. This, Evans-Pritchard suggested, is how all complex belief systems operate, even in the so-called scientific West. After all, the "scientific method" at its most stringent is hardly followed regularly by ordinary citizens, or even scientists once they are outside the laboratory. Evans-Pritchard's work has inspired many subsequent studies that debunk ethnocentric Western notions about the supposed irrationality of magic and religion.

Beliefs and practices bearing a resemblance to Azande witchcraft are found in many societies, in Africa and elsewhere. Comparative studies of these phenomena revealed interesting variation in the patterns of witchcraft accusations in a given society. Patterns of accusation fall into two basic types: witches are evil outsiders, or witches are internal enemies, either members of a rival faction or dangerous deviants.

These different patterns of accusation have different effects on the structure of the society in which they are made. If the witch is an evil outsider, witchcraft accusations can strengthen in-group ties as the group unites in opposition to the witch. If the witch is an internal enemy, however, accusations of witchcraft can weaken in-group ties, perhaps to the point at which one or more factions in a community might leave and build a new village; then the entire social structure may have to be rebuilt. This, anthropologists argued, was not really a bad thing, since what had prompted the accusations of witchcraft in the first place was a community that had grown too large for the prevailing political organization to maintain order. The witchcraft accusations provided a relatively nondestructive way to restore the community to the proper size for a kinship-based political system. If, on the other hand, the witch is a dangerous internal deviant, to accuse that person of witchcraft might be an attempt to control the deviant in defense of the wider values of the community.

religion = social cultural institutions

5.5 Religious Practitioners

Anthropologists also have devoted attention to the organization of religion as a social and cultural institution. Virtually without exception, anthropologists have stressed that complex sets of religious beliefs and practices are not merely the by-products of idiosyncratic individual invention. Rather, they are the products of collective cultural construction, performing social and cultural tasks that involve far more than tending to the spiritual needs of supporters.

religion

The contrast between different kinds of religious institutions in different societies can be illustrated with reference to the existence and role of specialized religious practitioners. In many small-scale societies, specialized ritual knowledge or practice may simply belong to elders who perform required rituals for their kin. Other societies, however, do accord a special status to religious specialists, and anthropologists have classified them in two broad categories: shamans and priests. Shamans are part-time religious specialists commonly found in small-scale egalitarian societies. The term *shaman* itself comes from Siberia, and Siberian shamans constitute the prototype that anthropologists have used to classify similar religious specialists in many other societies. They are believed to have the power to contact powerful cosmic beings directly on behalf of others, sometimes by traveling to the cosmic realm to communicate with them. They often plead with those beings to help their people—by curing them, for example—and they may also bring back messages for them. In other cases, the shaman enters an altered state of consciousness to seek and remove the cause of an illness that is afflicting a person who has come for healing. In many societies, the training that a shaman receives is long and demanding and may involve the use of powerful psychotropic substances. The position of shaman may be dangerous. The effects of entering altered states of consciousness can be long-lasting. The power to contact cosmic beings or to heal is itself perceived as ambiguous in many societies: the person who can intervene for good can also intervene for ill, and shamans are sometimes feared as well as admired.

shamans + priests carry out religious

shaman training - long and demanding

shamans are respected and feared for their talents

Priests - skilled in practice of religious rituals
trained to carry out rituals
• acts as mediator/communicator

Priests, by contrast, are skilled in the practice of religious rituals, which are carried out for the benefit of the group or individuals within the group. Priests frequently are full-time, formally trained specialists. They are found in hierarchical societies in which status differences between rulers and subjects are paralleled in the unequal relationship between priest and laity. Priests do not necessarily have direct contact with cosmic forces; rather, their major role is to mediate that contact successfully for their people by ensuring that the required rituals have been properly performed.

5.6 Change in Religious Systems

Change - and how a group cope,

Much ethnographic work has sought to describe and explain the details of particular religious systems, but the way change affects religious belief and practice has also been of great interest. When the members of a society are faced with drastic changes in their experiences—because of conquest, natural disaster, or radical dislocation (e.g., by migration)—they frequently seek new interpretations that will help them cope with the changes. In some cases, the individuals or groups in question will adopt an entirely new worldview, frequently a religious system, in the process of **conversion.** But in other cases, the result is a creative synthesis of old religious practices and new ones introduced from the outside, often by force, in a process called **syncretism.** Recently, some anthropologists have pointed out that most studies of religious syncretism have not paid sufficient attention to the unequal relationships between the parties that are syncretizing. Many have assumed that the worldview that changes most is the one belonging to the group with the least power. In some cases, syncretistic practices may indeed be introduced from above by powerful outsiders trying to ease tensions by deliberately making room for local beliefs. In other cases, however, syncretism can be seen as a way of resisting new ideas imposed from outside and above, masking old practices under the labels of the new imported ones.

conversion - adopting a new view

syncretism - mix of old and new practices

Sometimes social groups struggling with change defend or refashion their own way of life in a process that anthropologists

syncretism -
resisting new ideas
masking old practices under new labels

Revitalization — organized attempt by members of a soc. to create a more satisfying culture.

call **revitalization**: a deliberate, organized attempt by some members of a society to create a more satisfying culture. Revitalization movements arise in times of crisis, most often among groups facing oppression and radical transformation, usually at the hands of outsiders (e.g., colonizing powers). Revitalization may take a syncretistic form, but syncretism also may be rejected in favor of *nativism*, a return to the old ways. Some nativistic movements anticipate a messiah or prophet who will bring back a lost golden age of peace, prosperity, and harmony, a process often called *revivalism, millenarianism,* or *messianism.*

nativism

return to old ways

In recent years, anthropologists have examined not only the power relations involved in syncretism and revitalization but also the way different worldviews are related to the creation and maintenance of power relations within societies. For example, power differences may be sustained by differential knowledge, as when some groups of people within a society have access to important knowledge that is not available to everyone or when a limited number of individuals exercise control over key symbols and ritual practices. In many cases, those with power in the society seem to have successfully made use of the self-evident truths embodied in their worldview to continue to control others.

Change can occur when some groups of people have knowledge in group.

5.7 Summary

In this chapter, we considered how anthropologists define religion and the different kinds of religious systems they have defined. We also looked at anthropological approaches to myth, ritual, and witchcraft and at the religious practitioners that anthropologists have identified. We concluded by looking at the processes of religious change.

For Further Reading

GENERAL ANTHROPOLOGICAL WORKS ON RELIGION

Bowen 1998a; Child and Child 1993; Klass 1995; Wallace 1966

READINGS ON RELIGION

Bowen 1998b; Hicks 1999; Lambek 2002; Lehman and Myers 1996

6

The Dimensions of Social Organization

The key terms and concepts covered in this chapter, in the order in which they appear:

society

status

role

ascribed status

achieved status

social structure

institutions

social organization

functionalism

mechanical solidarity

organic solidarity

egalitarian societies

stratified societies

rank societies

sodalities

age set

age grades

secret societies

caste

social mobility

class

bourgeoisie

proletariat

clientage

patron-client
    relationships

compadrazgo

fictive kin

state

bureaucracy

race

ethnic group

ethnocide

genocide

sex

gender

postmodernism

berdache

ONE OF THE BASIC CLAIMS of anthropology is that human beings are a social species; that is, we have evolved to live with, and depend upon, others of our own species. Biological anthropologists have demonstrated, for example, that human infants are born earlier in the gestational process than are infants of apes and monkeys and that our young are dependent on other members of the group for far longer (fifteen to twenty years and more) before they are capable of establishing themselves as mature adults. Human interdependence means that we cannot survive as lone individuals but need to live with others; that is, we must live in **society.** When anthropologists speak of human society, at minimum they mean a group of human beings living together whose interactions with one another are patterned in regular ways. Such organized groups might also be identified by the particular geographical territory they inhabit, by the particular language they speak, or by the particular customs they follow—any or all of these features might distinguish them from other, neighboring societies. Such distinctive features, in turn, are mostly cultural, which is why anthropologists developed the habit of speaking as if each identifiable society came equipped with its own culture, and vice versa. Still, anthropologists recognize that no culture is monolithic, that cultural patterns may be borrowed or shared by people in different societies, and that a single society may contain within it representatives of different cultural traditions.

6.1 What Is Social Organization?

Anthropologists, together with other social scientists, have developed a set of analytic concepts that help describe and explain the orderly interdependence of human life in society. In particular, they have noted that people who interact in society do so not as unique individuals but as incumbents of publicly recognized social

status role on plays in society

positions. Each such social position is called a **status**, and all individuals come to occupy a range of different statuses in the course of their lives as they take part in a variety of social interactions.

People know what to do in such interactions because each status is associated with a corresponding **role:** a bundle of rights and obligations appropriate for occupants of the status in question. Thus, for example, the kinship status of *parent* might include, among other things, the right to discipline one's children and the obligation to feed them and send them to school. Violation of the role requirements associated with a particular social status generally brings about disapproval from other members of society.

Social scientists also distinguish two basic kinds of social statuses found in all societies: ascribed and achieved. An **ascribed status** is a status over which you have little control: you are born into it or grow into it. Anthropologists often use examples from human kinship systems to illustrate ascribed status. When you are born, you are automatically your parent's child, son or daughter; when you have children of your own, you automatically become a parent, mother or father. Such ascribed statuses ordinarily cannot be discarded, and any person who qualifies will be expected to fulfill the role obligations that go with the status. Very different, however, is an **achieved status,** one that you may not assume until or unless you meet certain criteria through your own (or others') efforts. For instance, being a college graduate is an achieved status, and achieving that status ordinarily requires both hard work and financial resources. Each member of a society occupies a mix of ascribed and achieved statuses.

ascribed status = born into it or grow into it

achieved status = one that you work for

Statuses and their accompanying roles are not isolated but are often linked to one another in complementary pairs or sets. For example, the statuses of parents and children (or mother and daughter, father and son, mother and son, or father and daughter) are reciprocal relationships. Thus, the right of parents to discipline their children matches the obligation of children to obey their parents (in theory, at least). To describe such a cluster of statuses with complementary roles is to begin to identify key enduring social relationships that provide a foundation for regularized, patterned social interaction, or **social structure.** But social structure is not simply a matter of interlinked and complementary statuses and roles attached to individuals. Most societies regularly associate particular sets of statuses with particular social groups defined in such terms as gender, family, lineage, clan, occupation, and political or religious affiliation. The relationships that link members of these various social groups may also be highly structured, often around a common task or cultural focus. The clusters of social statuses and groups that share such a common focus usually are called **institutions.** Thus, we speak of educational institutions that unite individuals and groups whose social statuses focus on educational issues or of political institutions that bring together individuals and groups whose statuses focus on the allocation of power in the society. Sometimes social structure refers only to the arrangement of status positions and groups with respect to each other. By contrast, social organization refers to the interlocking role relationships that are activated when statuses have incumbents and groups have members, all of whom are going about the daily business of living.

All this terminology is associated with the school of social scientific thought called **functionalism** (for more about functionalism, see Chapter 12). Functionalism was at its most influential in the early twentieth century and has since been much criticized, but many anthropologists and sociologists continue to find its terminology useful for describing basic social relations, even when they do not accept some of its more elaborate assumptions.

6.2 Dimensions of Social Organization

One issue of great interest in the early years of anthropology and sociology was the contrast between large and powerful European nation-states, with industrial technology and a complex division of labor, and small-scale societies, with little or no social stratification, whose members used simple tools to make a living and who were socially organized almost entirely on the basis of kinship. The contrast was sometimes phrased as an opposition between so-called civilized and so-called primitive societies. Sociologists were supposed to explain how "civilized" societies worked, and anthropologists were supposed to explain how "primitive" societies worked.

One widely influential model was proposed by Emile Durkheim (1858–1917), a French sociologist considered a founder of both modern sociology and modern anthropology. Durkheim was interested in what held a society together, contrasting societies held together by mechanical solidarity with those held together by organic solidarity. Mechanical solidarity characterized small-scale, kinship-based societies, in which all the tasks necessary for survival were carried out on a family level and families stayed together because they shared the same language and customs.

However, because kin groups were more-or-less self-sufficient in terms of meeting their survival needs, they could split off from one another relatively easily. Thus, mechanical solidarity could not bind together large numbers of people over long periods of time. **Organic solidarity,** by contrast, characterized large-scale societies, such as nation-states. In such societies, the tasks necessary for survival became specialties of different subgroups in a complex division of labor. For example, because those who specialized in pot making or metalworking might not have had the time or resources to produce their own food or clothing, they became dependent on other specialists—food producers or tailors—for these goods and services. Such interdependence meant that any single occupational grouping could not easily break away from the larger social whole, since it was not self-sufficient. Like the organ systems of a living body, specialized subgroups of complex societies clung together and depended on one another to survive, thereby preserving the overall health and strength of the whole. Thus, organic solidarity could hold much larger societies together far more securely than could mechanical solidarity.

Anthropologists incorporated concepts like these into their own analytic toolkit as they attempted to make sense of the variety of forms that different human societies assumed in different times and places. They also introduced new concepts to highlight further distinctions revealed by ethnographic research. One of the most basic is the fourfold classification of societies on the

Marginalia (handwritten):
* pol organization → band, tribe, chiefdom, state
* economic → foragers, herders, agriculturalists

basis of their form of political organization: band, tribe, chiefdom, and state (discussed at greater length in Chapter 7). Another is the very similar fourfold classification of societies on the basis of their form of economic organization: foragers, herders, extensive agriculturalists, and intensive agriculturalists (discussed at greater length in Chapter 8). The correlations between these different classifications highlight the connections between the ways people make a living and the ways they organize themselves politically.

The correlation is not perfect, however, and this is highlighted by another pair of concepts that crosscuts the earlier classifications. That is, anthropologists distinguish between **egalitarian societies,** in which all members (or component groups) enjoy roughly the same degree of wealth, power, and prestige, and **stratified societies,** in which some members (or component groups) have greater (and often permanent) access to some or all of these three valued resources. But the history of the transition from egalitarian societies (bands and tribes, in the current classification) to stratified societies (chiefdoms and states) is not fully understood. Some anthropologists pay particular attention to societies known through ethnography or history or archaeology in which egalitarian relations have begun to erode but in which permanent, inherited patterns of social stratification have not yet been established. Such societies, like those of the indigenous peoples of the northwest coast of North America or the Trobriand Islanders of Papua New Guinea, depended on foraging or extensive agriculture for subsistence, just as many egalitarian societies do. But they also have social structures that elevate certain individuals and their families above everyone else, allowing them privileged access to a limited number of high-status positions. Anthropologist Morton Fried called these **rank societies,** some of whose members ranked above others in social honor but did not have disproportionate access to wealth or power. The consensus is that fully stratified societies probably developed out of rank societies, but the exact mechanisms for the transition have been much debated and may well have been somewhat different in each case.

Ethnographic evidence supported Durkheim's observation that small-scale societies tend to be organized primarily on the

Marginalia (handwritten):
egalitarian societies - all members have same wealth power

stratified societies greater - permanent access to all 3 resources - Not equal!

Rank Societies social honor ranked higher - not a better access to wealth or power

3rd World

basis of kinship. As we discuss in Chapter 9, kinship systems must be fairly elaborate to carry out this task, and anthropology traditionally has sought to understand and compare the many different kinship systems that human beings have devised. However, even egalitarian societies whose social organization centered on kinship often invented additional forms of social organization that crosscut kinship groups and bound their members together at a more inclusive level; anthropologists often refer to such groups as sodalities. *- cut kinship groups - bound members together*

Sodalities can take many forms. Among the best known *@ inclusive level* ethnographically are the age-set systems from eastern Africa and the secret societies from western Africa. Found in such societies as the Nyakyusa living in present-day Tanzania, an **age set** is made up of a group of young men born within a specific time span, such *grouped by age* as five years; thus, a new age set is formed regularly every five years. Age sets typically progress through a sequence of statuses, or **age grades,** as their members grow older. There might be three age grades through which every age set must pass—for example, a junior, senior, and elder grade. Promotion from one age grade to the next typically is marked by rituals. Many societies with age-set systems devote particular attention to the *initiation* ritual that transforms boys into adult men, but societies differ in the degree of ritual elaboration with which they surround the passage of different sets from one grade to the next. Age-set systems have played different roles in different societies as well. Those sets belonging to junior age grades frequently have been characterized as *warriors,* but it is important to recognize that their activities as fighters or raiders often were subject to the control of men in senior age grades. Moreover, members of societies with age sets and age grades frequently use the age-grade structure as a way of thinking about time and attempting to regulate its passage by ritual means.

The Mende, Sherbro, Kpelle, and other neighboring peoples who today live in the western African nation-states of Sierra Leone, Ivory Coast, Liberia, and Guinea developed **secret societies** as forms of social organization that crosscut kinship groupings. Some secret societies admit only men as members, others admit only women, and at least one admits both men and women. Only

* Secret societies cross-cut kinship. groupings

adults may belong to secret societies, and children must undergo initiation rituals in order to achieve that status and gain admittance; some anthropologists have undergone initiation as part of their research. The "secret" part of secret societies refers to the special knowledge revealed only to initiates, which they are not allowed to share with outsiders. Initiates may also progress to higher positions within the society to which they belong, but they must pay fees and receive special instruction to do so. In addition to these internal activities, secret societies also carry out specific tasks in public. Social relations between men and women tend to be highly egalitarian in cultures with secret societies; for example, the male Poro society and female Sande society of a village might jointly be responsible for supervising public behavior and sanctioning those who violate expected rules of conduct.

Forms of social organization, such as kinship and sodalities, can still be found in societies that are socially stratified, but their scope and importance is modified by new features of social structure that sustain the inequalities on which social stratification is based. That is, stratified societies are internally divided into a number of groups that are arranged in a hierarchy. The two most important such hierarchical structures studied by anthropologists have been caste and class.

6.3 Caste and Class

Anthropologists traditionally describe **caste** societies as stratified societies in which membership in a particular ranked subgroup is ascribed at birth and in which **social mobility,** or movement by individuals out of the subgroup in which they were born, is not allowed. Although the original prototype for caste societies comes from India, anthropologists have used the term to describe similar social arrangements in other societies.

In India and elsewhere in South Asia, each caste traditionally is defined not only as the endogamous group within which members must choose mates (see Chapter 10 for a definition of endogamy) but also in terms of a traditional occupation with which the caste is identified (salt maker, farmer, warrior, priest, etc.). Each occupation, and the caste associated with it, is ranked on a scale of purity and pollution, with higher-ranked castes subject to various dietary and other taboos required to maintain caste purity. Highest on the purity scale are the *Brahmins,* the vegetarian priestly caste, and lowest are the out-castes or untouchables, who eat meat and whose occupations (leatherworker, street sweeper) regularly bring them into contact with polluting substances such as dead animals and excrement. Recent studies of caste societies have demonstrated that the high ritual status of the Brahmin caste does not mean that Brahmins dominate the caste system; rather, these studies emphasize the centrality of the king and his warrior caste, the *Ksatriya.* Kings could determine the relative rank of local castes, for example, and from the king's perspective, the function of these other castes, including the Brahmins, was to protect him from pollution. By the end of the twentieth century, caste relations had undergone significant modification in urban India: castes close in rank sometimes came together in political alliances, and members of the same caste but from different regions of the country (e.g., Brahmins) came together to build solidarity on a national level. Unfortunately, Indian cities have also been the site of caste violence in recent years, when members of more favorably situated castes clash with those struggling to escape from a permanent position at the bottom of the caste hierarchy.

Social class, by contrast, is the term anthropologists use to describe ranked subgroups in a stratified society whose members are differentiated from one another primarily in economic terms, either on the basis of income level or, as Karl Marx (1818–83) proposed, on the basis of the kind of property owned by members of different classes. In an industrial capitalist society, for example, Marx argued that class divisions had formed between the **bourgeoisie,** or capitalist class, which owned the means of production (tools, knowledge, raw materials), and the **proletariat,** or working class, which owned only their labor power, which they sold to bourgeois factory owners in exchange for cash wages (see Chapters 8 and 11 for further discussion of these terms). Either way, members of some social classes are seen to have privileged access to material resources, while the access of members of other classes to these resources is more or less severely restricted. Moreover, ruling classes use their privileged situation to dominate less powerful classes.

Traditionally, anthropologists have distinguished class from caste on the grounds that social classes are not closed and social mobility from one class into another is not forbidden. An emphasis on class mobility tends to highlight exceptional, successful individuals who have moved from lower to higher classes, while overlooking the enduring rigidity of class boundaries for most people in many societies (Great Britain, for example) as well as cases of downward class mobility. At the same time, emphasizing the inability of individuals in a caste system to move from a lower-ranked to a higher-ranked caste overlooks the ways in which permanent members of different castes sometimes collectively succeed in elevating the relative position of their caste within the overall caste system.

The members of ranked subgroups in stratified societies do not always accept the position they are supposed to occupy in a class or caste hierarchy, and struggles between such groups do occur. Marx, in particular, emphasized the class antagonism between bourgeoisie and proletariat, which he predicted ultimately would produce class warfare in which the workers would overthrow the capitalist order and establish socialism. Anthropologists working in India have challenged the view that people occupying the lowest ranks in the caste system necessarily accept their low status as right and proper. Indeed, the caste violence that has occasionally erupted in Indian cities in recent decades testifies to the unwillingness of those at the bottom of the system to accept such a position. At the same time, interactions between individuals from different levels of a hierarchical social system is not regularly characterized by such violence, and members of different ranked groups find nonviolent ways to establish relationships with one another. If different groups are associated with different occupations, their members may have only impersonal contact with one another when they need one another's services—for example, in the workplace. But many societies have developed institutionalized cross-hierarchy connections that allow individuals belonging to differently ranked groups to create a more per-

integrating different classes

sonalized relationship. Anthropologists often call such connections (clientage) or patron-client relationships, since they normally involve a member of a high-ranking group (the patron) and a member of a low-ranking group (the client). A well-documented example of clientage is the Latin American institution of *compadrazgo,* or coparenthood. Such a relationship may be created when a low-ranking married couple (the clients) asks a high-ranking individual (the patron) to serve as their child's *compadre,* or godparent, at the child's baptism. If the patron agrees and participates in the baptism ritual, then that individual and the child's parents will have a new relationship. They will call each other by the kin terms *compadre* or *comadre,* and their relationship will become less formal and more friendly. Because they are now *compadres,* the child's parents will feel freer to approach their patron *(compadre/comadre)* when they are in trouble, and he or she will be morally obliged to help them out. Conversely, if their patron needs supporters (e.g., in politics), they ordinarily will feel obligated to supply that support. Because clientage institutions like *compadrazgo* frequently remake the relationship of unrelated individuals on the model of formal kinship, anthropologists sometimes describe *compadres* as **fictive kin.** *"adopting" relationship*

Stratified societies with large populations and a complex division of labor ordinarily are associated with the political form called the **state** (discussed in more detail in Chapter 7). The organic solidarity of state societies is maintained by a new kind of institution neither present nor needed in small-scale, egalitarian societies: bureaucracy. A **bureaucracy** is a hierarchically organized set of formal statuses, each of which is associated with a highly specific role and all of which are designed to work together to ensure the smooth functioning of complex organizations such as state governments or business corporations. Ideally, bureaucrats defend the avowed purposes of the organizations they serve, and much of their work involves following proper procedures in performing the particular tasks for which they are responsible. Complex organizations could not function without bureaucracies, but the formality and complexity of bureaucratic procedures often frustrates outsiders and may tempt bureaucrats to manipulate their positions for their own personal benefit.

Upper and lower class – bridging the gap.

complex organizations have bureaucracy

Descriptions in terms of caste or class may be useful in tracing the gross outlines of the structure of complex stratified societies, but they are rarely sufficient to characterize all the significant dimensions of social organization found in such societies. Anthropologists recognize the importance of additional categories used by members of these societies that may be embedded within or may crosscut caste or class structures. With this in mind, they also have long paid attention to the category of race and have grown increasingly interested in distinctions framed in terms of ethnic identity, gender, and sexual preference.

6.4 Race

The concept of **race** was deeply intertwined with the very origin of anthropology as a discipline (see discussion in Chapter 2). Although some late-nineteenth-century physical anthropologists hoped to demonstrate a causal connection between the physical attributes of a group and their language and customs, early-twentieth-century anthropologists worked hard to expose the flaws in such attempts. The modern concept of culture was developed to explain how individuals could learn *any* language or culture, regardless of their biological origins, and to argue against schemes that tried to classify the world's peoples into mutually exclusive races and to rank them hierarchically.

At the same time, the absence of any biological basis for racial categories has never prevented people in some societies from inventing *cultural* categories based on a group's supposed origins or physical appearance and then using such categories as building blocks for their social institutions. Precisely because racial categories are culturally constructed on the basis of superficial appearances, however, different societies may draw the boundaries around racially defined social groups in different ways.

For example, as the twenty-first century dawns, people living in the United States tend to classify people into several different racial categories, but the great divide remains between two major racial categories, black and white. The enslavement of Africans by Europeans in the United States and the continued oppression of their descendants even after emancipation in the nineteenth century have created a social reality for residents of the United States in which the divide between black and white appears so obvious as to be beyond question. To be sure, continued world domination by societies whose ruling groups trace their origins to Europe has sustained a global hierarchy in which light skin is valued over dark skin. And yet, outside the United States, in the Caribbean or in Brazil, where Africans also suffered under European slavery, race is understood in different ways. Rather than an unchanging identity that people carry around with them everywhere they go, the racial identity one claims, or is accorded by others, may vary from situation to situation, depending on who else is present. That is, in any particular social setting, those with the lightest skin may claim, and be accorded, the identity of "white," but when they move into a different setting and interact with others whose skin is lighter than theirs, they may have to accept being assigned to one of a variety of lower-status, nonwhite categories. Some anthropologists use the term *colorism* to describe this pattern of racial classification, in contrast to the once-and-for-all pattern of racial classification found in the United States.

Moreover, social mobility and the cultural changes that accompany it—learning the dominant language, getting an education, finding gainful employment, adopting new customs in diet and dress—may be interpreted as movement from one racial group into another. Thus, in some parts of Latin America, indigenous people who cut their hair, speak Spanish, wear European clothing, get an education, and find Western-style occupations may be classified by other members of their society as "white" or "mixed" rather than "indigenous," even though their outward biological features have not altered. Anthropologists sometimes use the term *social race* to describe these cases, in which so-called racial labels are used to refer to cultural rather than physical differences between groups.

6.5 Ethnicity

The distinction between classifications based on biology and on culture is thus not clear-cut. This highlights the ways that people can emphasize or downplay any of a wide range of physical and cultural attributes, either to define an identity for themselves or to assign an identity to others. This ambiguity appears when we consider another important social category investigated by anthropologists, that of the **ethnic group**. Ethnic groups usually are distinguished from other kinds of social groups based on attributes defining group membership that are cultural in nature: shared language, shared religion, shared customs, shared history. However, because all this cultural sharing could never have occurred if group members did not regularly interact, and even intermarry, ethnic identity is often thought, by both group members and outsiders, to be rooted in some common biological origin. Indeed, some anthropologists think of racial identity as being no different from ethnic identity, except that racial identity supposedly is biological in origin while ethnic identity has a cultural origin. And in practice, the concepts of both race and ethnic group often overlap with the concept of nation (discussed in more detail in Chapter 7).

[margin note: racial identity = biological in origin ↔ ethnic identity = cultural origin]

All such cultural identities—whether understood in terms of kinship or race or ethnic identity—develop in opposition to other, similar identities in a complex social setting. Thus, the boundaries that eventually come to be recognized between races or ethnic groups are a product of both internal self-definition and external definition by others. Of course, a sense of group belonging, and the ability to distinguish one's own group from neighboring groups, stretches far back into the human past. What makes the study of racial or ethnic or national identity so important today, however, is the new role such groups take on within the boundaries of contemporary nation-states.

As discussed in Chapter 7, nation-states are relatively new forms of political organization, first developing in late-eighteenth-century and nineteenth-century Europe and the Americas and later spreading throughout the globe following the dissolution of Western colonial empires. Before the French Revolution, European states were ruled by kings and emperors whose access to the throne was officially believed to have been ordained by God. After the French Revolution, which thoroughly discredited the divine right of kings and proclaimed the "Rights of Man," a new basis for legitimate state authority had to be found. Over the course of the nineteenth century, the notion developed that rulers were legitimate only if they ruled over other members of the nation to which they themselves belonged.

When legitimacy began to depend on the perfect overlap of nation and state, on a recognized bond of cultural or linguistic or religious—that is, national—identity between ruler and ruled, the persistence of groups with different forms of identity within the boundaries of the nation-state became problematic. If such groups successfully resisted assimilation into the nation that the state was supposed to represent, their existence called into question the legitimacy of the state and its rulers. Indeed, if their numbers were sufficient, they might well claim that they were a separate nation, entitled to a state of their own! This situation describes much contemporary political life at the turn of the twenty-first century, when ruling regimes in more and more nation-states, fearful of losing stability and legitimacy in the eyes of the world, engaged in violence against all citizens who challenged their right to rule. **Ethnocide** (the destruction of a culture) and **genocide** (the physical extermination of an entire people) have often been the result, generating movements of refugee and immigrant populations whose social and political status is often anomalous and ambiguous in a world of nation-states.

In recent years, anthropologists have paid particular attention to the ways in which oppressed racial and ethnic groups, whether resident or immigrant, have struggled to mobilize their members to resist oppression. This has occurred in countries all over the world, including those of Europe and North America. As forces of globalization have weakened nation-states and promoted the flow of large numbers of people of various backgrounds into societies different from their own, new ethnic contacts and ethnic frictions have developed.

6.6 Gender

These global ethnic phenomena are a striking illustration of the way in which contemporary cultural developments have led anthropologists to rethink many long-held assumptions. But some anthropologists might argue that even further reaching has been the continuing impact of feminism on social science scholarship. In the early decades of the twentieth century, most ethnographies, including those written by women, were based primarily on the views of male informants, even concerning matters pertaining to women. Thus, most discussions of "the culture" of a group in fact portrayed culture from the viewpoint of men (often high-status men). When women were discussed at all, it was usually in the context of marriage and the family, and the assumption seemed to be that women's cultural roles as wives and mothers followed "naturally" from the biological facts of pregnancy and lactation. Margaret Mead's demonstration in the 1930s of the lack of correlation between biological sex and culturally expected behaviors of males and females in society was a well-known exception to this pattern.

Beginning in the 1960s, however, feminist anthropologists forced a serious reexamination of traditional assumptions about the roles of women and men in human society. Their first success was to present overwhelming ethnographic evidence showing that the cultural roles of women and men in any society could not be predicted from or reduced to their biological anatomy. It has thus become commonplace in cultural anthropology to use the term sex to refer to the physical characteristics that distinguish males from females (e.g., body shape, distribution of body hair, reproductive organs, sex chromosomes). By contrast, **gender** is used to refer to the culturally constructed roles assigned to males or females, and these vary considerably from society to society. Early feminist anthropology emphasized, as Mead had done, that gender and biological sex did not correlate.

As feminist anthropologists began examining past ethnographies for gender bias, they also encouraged new ways of doing research and writing ethnography that explored women and their activities in *all* areas of life, not merely marriage and family. Anthropologists now commonly acknowledge that "the culture" of any particular group may well look different to women than it does to men, and they bring this awareness to their own fieldwork and ethnographic writing.

[Handwritten margin notes:]
Sex = biological difference
gender = culturally constructed roles assigned to males/ females

The thoroughgoing reconsideration of traditional anthropological concepts promoted by feminists, ethnic minorities, indigenous peoples, and others in recent years can be placed within the
context of the larger intellectual critique of modernity, including
modern scientific rationality, that has been called **postmodernism**
(discussed in Chapters 1 and 12). Much postmodern criticism has
been directed at concepts that are presumed to capture the universal essences of objects, relationships, or processes in the world.
Thus, feminist anthropologists have struggled to debunk the supposed universal "truths" about women, showing that "women"
was itself a problematic category that flattened out all the many
different ways in which human persons with a female reproductive anatomy might live their lives. Women of different races and
classes and ethnic groups, it has been shown, often lead very different lives within the same "culture." The categories of "race"
and "class" and "ethnic group" can also be seen as problematic,
since the experiences of, for example, men and women belonging
to the same race, class, or ethnic group are also very different
from one another. Moreover, the relevance of one's ethnic identity,
as well as one's willingness to acknowledge it, has been shown to
differ in different social settings.

6.7 Sexual Preference

In recent years, one of the most important attempts to pick apart
the supposed essence of a cultural category has been made by
anthropologists and other social scientists exploring the highly
controversial topic of sexual preference. Same-sex sexual practices
have become an accepted topic for research in anthropology. One
result has been that the traditionally unquestioned "normality" of
heterosexual sexual practices has been called into question, and
the culturally variable links between biological anatomy, gender
identity, and sexual preference have been explored in a variety of
ethnographic contexts. In a manner parallel to the development of
feminist anthropology, legitimation of "homosexuality" as a practice and as a topic of study was followed by critiques highlighting
the Western male bias tacitly attached to the term. As a result, the

varieties of "homosexual" experience in Western societies have been scrutinized, allowing the recognition of important differences in the experiences of gay, lesbian, bisexual, and transgendered individuals. These studies have been supplemented not only by ethnographic research on similar topics in other cultures but also by a reexamination of older ethnographic writings about societies in which nonheterosexual practices have been institutionalized. In this regard, anthropologists have given particular attention to research and writing on the cultural and sexual practices of the so-called berdache. *berdache - men allowed to take on*

The term **berdache** traditionally has been used in anthropology *activities* to refer to indigenous (especially Native American) social roles in *of the* which men (and sometimes women) were allowed to take on the *opposite* activities, and sometimes the dress, of members of the opposite sex. *sex* Sometimes berdache is defined as "male transvestite," but this definition is inadequate because it ignores the fact that a man who took on other aspects of a woman's role might also, as women did, establish sexual relationships with men. Indeed, the term meant "male prostitute" to the early French explorers in the Americas who first used it to describe the men they observed engaging in such behavior.

Today, many gay and lesbian anthropologists refuse to use the term, as do many contemporary members of indigenous societies who view themselves as modern embodiments of these alternative-gender roles. Some have proposed using terms like *third gender* or *two spirit* instead, although no consensus has yet been achieved. As ethnographic research on alternative-gender roles and sexual practices in a wide variety of societies accumulates, a more adequate set of analytic concepts is likely to be developed. At present, this research continues to generate controversy, not only in societies whose members condemn nonheterosexual intercourse but also among anthropologists whose theoretical and personal views on sexuality are not easily reconciled.

6.8 Summary

In this chapter, we considered the various ways that human beings have devised to manage human interdependence. We looked at how status and role are defined, at the different kinds of stratified and nonstratified social arrangements that people employ, and at class, caste, race, ethnicity, gender, and sexual preference as dimensions of social organization.

For Further Reading

GENDER/SEXUALITY

Blackwood and Wieringa 1999; Bonvillain 1995; Di Leonardo 1991; Gutmann 1997; Herdt 1994; Miller 1993; Stone 1997; Suggs and Miracle 1993; Weston 1993

SOCIAL ORGANIZATION

Fried 1967; Graburn 1971

ETHNICITY

Williams 1989

COLONIALISM

Pels 1997

RACE

Smedley 1999

GENOCIDE AND ETHNOCIDE

Messer 1993; Nagengast 1994

7 Political Anthropology

The key terms and concepts covered in this chapter, in the order in which they appear:

power
state
political anthropologists
politics

coercive power
persuasive power

political ecology
ecological anthropology
political economy

raiding
feuding
mediator
negotiation
bloodwealth
warfare

egalitarian
band
tribes
chiefdoms

social stratification
caste
class
slaves
sumptuary
wealth
prestige

complex societies
acephalous
consensus

headman
big man

statuses
roles
authority
bureaucracy
formalization
sanctions

law
substantive law
procedural law
civil law
criminal law
law codes
courts
adjudicate
crime

nationalism
nation
nation-states
imagined community

domination
hegemony
ideology
hidden transcripts

WHEN NINETEENTH-CENTURY ethnologists from Europe and North America began to compare societies across space and over time, they noticed not only that members of different societies made a living in different ways but also that daily life in all these varied societies seemed to unfold in an orderly and predictable manner. The presence of apparent social order in societies of different sizes, organized according to a variety of diverse social principles, puzzled some observers because of their own assumptions about what made social order possible. These ethnologists lived in societies whose leaders assumed that individual human beings were naturally selfish and competitive, and thus could live peaceably together only if they were compelled to do so by threat of physical force. That is, they believed that social order was not natural but could result only from the external imposition of power.

7.1 Power

Power often has been understood first and foremost in terms of physical coercion, especially by European philosophers and social scientists, who traditionally define power in terms of one individual's ability to compel others to do what he or she wants them to do. This view of power seemed natural in societies like those of Europe and America that were organized into states. Anthropologists agree that states were not invented in Europe but first appeared several thousand years ago in half a dozen different regions of the world. Anthropologists group these states together, ancient and modern, because they appear to share certain prototypical features. That is, for anthropologists, a **state** is an independent political entity that controls a geographical territory with clear boundaries and that defends itself from external threats with an army and from internal disorder with police. States have specialized institutions to raise revenue by collecting taxes and to carry out other public duties, such as maintaining roads and markets. All of these tasks become possible because the state monopolizes the legitimate use of physical force.

Certainly, European history, following the religious wars of the sixteenth and seventeenth centuries and the revolutions of the late eighteenth and nineteenth centuries, seemed to prove that nothing less than deadly force in the hands of a strong state will keep people in line. Without the state, according to seventeenth-century philosopher Thomas Hobbes, life was supposed to be "nasty, brutish, and short." And yet, historical and ethnographic materials suggested strongly that, elsewhere in the world, many societies not organized into states had long been able to conduct their external and internal affairs in an orderly fashion. Could it be that power was successfully institutionalized in these societies in forms other than the state?

These kinds of questions have traditionally been asked by **political anthropologists.** These scholars share with political philosophers and political scientists an interest in **politics:** the ways in which power relations (particularly unequal power relations) affect human social affairs. Political anthropologists have paid particular attention to how members of different societies go about making public decisions that affect the society as a whole. They also are interested in why people either accept these decisions as right and proper or criticize them as wrong and improper. Political anthropologists compare how leadership is understood and exercised, how competition between rivals is regulated, and how disputes are settled. In all these areas, people's cultural beliefs and practices clearly play a large role. In recent years, increasing attention has been focused on the ways in which larger regional and global power relations shape opportunities for the exercise of power by local groups (see additional discussion of global issues in Chapter 11).

To study all these dimensions of power requires a view of power that does not limit it merely to **coercive power,** or the use of physical force. For many anthropologists, a more useful definition of power would be a generalized capacity to transform. From this point of view, coercion is only one kind of power, and attention must be paid to all those other forms of influence that transform people's practical activities or their ideas about the world *without* relying on physical force. Forms of **persuasive power** range from the charisma of a religious prophet, to the formally proscribed but ubiquitous ability of weaker members of society to manipulate social rules to promote their own well-being, to the outright refusal of compliance shown by factory workers who go on strike.

7.2 Political Ecology and Political Economy

As the latter example suggests, for anthropologists, political issues do not develop in a vacuum but are intimately related to other dimensions of collective life, especially economic matters. The intersection of politics and economics has been approached in two main directions by anthropologists. **Political ecology** pays attention to the ways in which human groups struggle with one another for control of (usually local) material resources. This approach fits within the broader orientation of **ecological anthropology**, which focuses on the relationships linking particular human populations and the immediate ecological settings to which they must adapt to survive (see additional discussion of populations and environments in Chapter 8). Although some political ecologists emphasize the way in which ecological factors shape the political struggle for resource control, others emphasize the way in which the outcome of political struggles determines which groups will have access to how much of which resources.

By contrast, other political anthropologists see their work as falling within the purview of what has been called **political economy**; that is, the focus is on the political creation (and consequences) of the division of labor in society. Political anthropologists studying non-Western societies that have been subject to colonial domination often find a focus on political economy useful. This perspective offers a framework for describing and explaining how capitalist colonialism disrupted indigenous precapitalist political and economic arrangements, reorganized relations of production, expropriated local wealth and power, and promoted the formation of new social classes.

7.3 Disputes and Dispute Resolution

One important focus of political anthropology has been on how the members of different societies, living within different kinds of economic and social institutions, handle their relations with their neighbors. Recall that a key task of the state as a political institution was to defend itself from external attack and from internal subversion. Anthropologists were curious about how societies not organized as states handled these matters. The ethnographic record shows that a variety of mechanisms, formal and informal, have been developed in different times and places. As they often have done when confronted with ethnographic variety, anthropologists invented classifications to sort out the patterns of dispute (and dispute resolution) about which they had information.

Scale is always important when considering these various mechanisms. Consider, for example, the issue of warfare. At the turn of the twenty-first century, when those of us who live in industrialized nation-states think about "warfare," we typically think of a conflict like World War I or World War II, in which the professional armies of two or more nation-states clash using modern weapons (machine guns, tanks, bombs, etc.). The war ends when one side concedes defeat, lays down its weapons, and agrees to formal, written terms of surrender. But such a model of warfare has almost nothing in common with the kinds of violent clashes more typically found in smaller-scale, nonindustrial societies without states. To make the differences plain, ethnologists worked out a set of categories that could distinguish modern warfare from these other kinds of conflict.

For example, violent conflicts can be distinguished from one another in terms of how long they last and what goals they are expected to achieve. **Raiding,** for instance, is defined as a short-term use of force with a limited goal, such as stealing a few head of cattle or other material goods, usually from a neighboring group. Pastoral peoples commonly resort to raiding to recover animals they believe are owed them or simply to increase the size of their own herds at the expense of a nearby group of herders. Raiding can be contrasted with **feuding,** which describes ongoing, chronic hostilities between groups of neighbors or kin. Feuds are politically destabilizing because they are potentially endless. Often a feud begins when a member of one kin group takes the life of a member of a neighboring kin group. Relatives of the dead person feel obliged to avenge the death of their kinsman or kinswoman and so vow to take the equivalent of "an eye for an eye, and a tooth for a tooth." In this way, feuding can be seen as a form of negative reciprocity (defined in Chapter 8). Feuding groups do not feel obliged to take the life of the specific individual who killed their relative; the death of any member of the group to which the killer belongs will restore the balance. But the group responsible for the first death will then feel obligated to avenge the death visited on them as repayment for the first death, and so on.

Peoples who engage in feuding are quite aware that this form of retaliation can escalate into a bloodbath. Therefore, some groups have invented cultural institutions that feuding groups can call upon to achieve settlement, such as a **mediator:** a formally recognized, neutral third party to whom the disputing parties can appeal to settle their differences. Mediators have no coercive power of their own but instead rely on the persuasive power of **negotiation**—that is, of verbal argument and compromise—to induce the hostile parties to come to a mutually acceptable resolution of their dispute. Mediators play an exceedingly important role when the parties to a feud are close neighbors who must somehow find a way to coexist despite their mutual grievances. Often mediators appeal to traditional practices designed to mollify the aggrieved party, such as an offer by the offending party of a given amount of material wealth (e.g., in livestock or other valuables), a payment frequently referred to as **bloodwealth.** Some anthropologists view the invention of bloodwealth as a major cultural achievement that for millennia has managed to short-circuit feuds and restrain their destructive capacity.

Warfare, by contrast, involves violent conflict on a significantly larger scale. Entire societies mobilize against each other, trying to kill as many members of the other society as possible until one side surrenders to the other. Warfare occurs when persuasive means of dispute resolution, such as diplomacy, either do not exist or have failed or are ignored, and physical combat becomes the only avenue open to settle differences. Of course, none of these classificatory labels is airtight; all of them are designed to highlight what appear to be salient similarities and differences from a political point of view. Real-life cases are always more complex and ambiguous than the labels themselves might suggest. For example, feuding carried out on a grand-enough scale begins to look a lot like warfare.

7.4 Forms of Political Organization

The contrast between feuding and warfare draws our attention back to an issue that has preoccupied so many political anthropologists: societies that engage in warfare typically have some form of centralized political organization, whereas societies that engage in feuding typically do not. Prehistorians and political anthropologists have compared the different political systems known from archaeology, history, and ethnography. Like the nineteenth-century evolutionists, they recognize four broad types of political systems that appear to have developed over the 200,000 or so years our species has existed and that correlate broadly with other cultural attributes, such as subsistence strategies and types of kinship organization (for discussion of subsistence strategies see Chapter 8; for kinship organization see Chapter 9). In the mid-twentieth century, anthropologists like Elman Service and Morton Fried offered new interpretations of cultural evolution that incorporated critiques of nineteenth-century schemes. Their work has influenced most subsequent anthropological discussions of comparative political systems.

The earliest political forms appear to have been **egalitarian;** that is, all (adult) members of the society had roughly equal access to valued resources, both material and social. The oldest human societies we know about archaeologically depended on foraging, and the egalitarian political form associated with this mode of subsistence has been called the **band.** Foraging societies are small in scale; historically and prehistorically, they were few in number and widely scattered across the land. Bands of foragers typically number no more than fifty individuals coresident at the same time. Tasks are assigned on the basis of gender and age, but the division is not rigid. Kinship systems are generally bilateral (defined in Chapter 9), and bands create alliances with one another through marriage. Relations of economic exchange are organized on the basis of reciprocity (defined in Chapter 8).

The domestication of plants and animals marked a major shift in the subsistence strategy, supporting somewhat larger egalitarian social groups that anthropologists call **tribes.** The major social change associated with those who took up *horticulture* (extensive agriculture) or those who began to herd animals is seen in the appearance of unilineal kinship groups (defined in Chapter 9) that became the joint owners of property in the form of farmland or herds. New cultural forms such as age grades (defined in Chapter 6) may create social links that crosscut kinship groups. Kin groups may compete with one another for resources, but they are not ranked hierarchically; indeed, within each kin group, the access of adults to communal resources remains broadly equal.

The first evidence of the erosion of egalitarian political forms is found in those societies organized as **chiefdoms.** Chiefdoms make use of the same forms of subsistence and kinship as tribes, but new social arrangements show the emergence of distinctions among lineages in terms of status or ranking. In particular, one lineage is elevated above the rest, and its leader (the chief) becomes a key political figure whose higher status often derives from his role in redistributive economic exchanges (defined in Chapter 8). The chief's higher rank (and that of the lineage to which he belongs) gives him an increased opportunity to favor his kin and his supporters with material or social benefits, but he has very limited coercive power. Significant power remains in the hands of lineages, who continue to control their own communal wealth in land or herds.

TABLE 7.1   Forms of Political Organization
Band
Tribe
Chiefdom
State

The social differentiation, ranking, and centralization that are incipient in chiefdoms are fully realized with the appearance of states. The state organization described previously (with its territory, army, police, tax collectors, and so forth) did not appear until well after the invention of intensive agriculture approximately 10,000 years ago, which generated surpluses that could be used to support full-time occupational specialists such as potters, weavers, metalworkers, priests, and kings.

7.5 Social Stratification

As well as monopolizing physical force, state organization enforces **social stratification;** a permanent, inherited inequality between the various component groups of which the society is composed. (Table 7.1 lists the basic forms of political organization.) Anthropologists frequently distinguish between **caste** societies, in which the members of distinct stratified groups are not allowed to move out of the stratum in which they were born, and **class** societies, in which some social mobility up or down the class hierarchy may occur (see Chapter 6 for details). At the very bottom of a class or caste hierarchy may be found a social category whose access to valued resources is so restricted that members do not even dispose of their own labor. Anthropologists often describe these individuals as **slaves.**

Stratification means that some groups have disproportionate access to valued resources. For example, high-ranking groups may have **sumptuary** privileges; that is, they may be the only members *state societies = complex societies*

of society entitled to wear certain fabrics or eat certain foods. In stratified societies, moreover, valued resources include not just material **wealth** (e.g., land or herds) or cultural **prestige** (e.g., esteem or respect) but also power itself. That is, those who rule the state are able to use their monopoly on coercive power to keep the lion's share of wealth and prestige and to perpetuate this inequality from one generation to the next. Because of the elaborate division of labor and its hierarchical organization in stratified castes or classes, state societies often are called **complex societies,** especially by archaeologists and prehistorians, who contrast them with the less elaborate and more egalitarian bands and tribes that preceded them chronologically.

Those political anthropologists interested in the evolution of the state frequently have speculated on the forces that could have been responsible for transforming egalitarian political relations that had endured for thousands of years into unequal political relations. Many different single, unique causes, or *prime movers,* have been proposed to account for the emergence of political inequality and centralized hierarchy (e.g., population pressure, dependency on irrigation, conquest by neighbors, and environmental circumscription, to name but a few). The consensus among contemporary prehistorians seems to be that no single factor can explain all cases in which inequality and centralization emerged from egalitarian political arrangements. For example, archaeologists have uncovered the remains of many early societies organized as chiefdoms that never developed into states. It seems clear that while certain underlying factors must have been present, contingent historical factors also played an important role.

Some anthropologists are further concerned that preoccupation with explaining the "rise of the state" smuggles back into the analysis assumptions of unilineal evolutionism that had supposedly been expunged long ago. Such a preoccupation can make a drive toward social complexity from band, to tribe, to chiefdom, to state seem inevitable and irresistible, even if the paths to complexity are varied and have not always been taken and even though human history is littered with the fall of states and the disintegration of empires. To the extent that states and empires and other encompassing forms of social complexity are seen as powerful generators of inequality and oppression, moreover, the rise of state control will not necessarily be viewed as progressive, and the disintegration of an empire may be viewed as liberating. Overall, the open-ended unpredictability of future sociopolitical changes can then be openly acknowledged, and more attention can be paid to the ways in which societies organized with different degrees of complexity can coexist with and reshape one another.

7.6 Forms of Political Activity

The classification of political systems as bands, tribes, chiefdoms, and states can be useful even if one is not interested in their possible evolutionary relationships. Many political anthropologists have used these categories as prototypes for distinct forms of political life and have been more interested in exploring how these forms actually work. Such anthropologists have been intrigued by the striking contrast between egalitarianism and inequality, between diffuseness of power in egalitarian societies and centralized monopoly of power in stratified societies. As Meyer Fortes and E. E. Evans-Pritchard put it more than fifty years ago, centralized societies like chiefdoms or states have *heads* (e.g., chiefs or kings or presidents), whereas uncentralized societies do not; that is, they are acephalous (without heads). As Fortes and Evans-Pritchard noted, acephalous societies were not politically chaotic, but political order in such societies clearly seemed to be the result of cultural mechanisms rather different from the mechanisms upon which centralized societies relied. Many anthropologists set about trying to identify just what those mechanisms were. To describe a band or tribe as "stateless" or "acephalous" is to describe it in terms of what it lacks: a state, or a head of state. As indicated previously, however, some anthropologists prefer to describe bands and tribes in terms of what they possess, which is a high degree of political equality accorded to all adults (or, sometimes, to all adult males). People in the United States or Europe tend to equate political equality with forms of electoral democracy. But to do so is misleading, because our forms of electoral democracy occur within the framework of a state, whereas the political equality found in egalitarian societies exists apart from the state.

To be sure, we find in bands and tribes many characteristics that might be justly described as "democratic"; for example, political decisions that affect the society as a whole must involve the consent of all the adults (or adult males) in the society. But members of egalitarian societies typically do not go to the polls to vote formally for or against a particular policy, with the understanding that whichever position gains the most votes wins. Instead, informal discussion and negotiation about alternatives take place among all adults who will be affected, a process that is feasible when the group is small, as is typical in most band and tribal societies. Eventually, a decision that all adult members of the society accept emerges from this process, a result known as **consensus.** This does not mean that consensus is easy to achieve. Precisely because no adult in an egalitarian society can force any other adult to do anything, negotiations require enormous verbal skill. Successful negotiators often employ a range of techniques, ranging from indirectly suggesting, to cajoling, to shaming, to predicting dire consequences for failure to comply. In all cases, we are referring here to the exercise of persuasive, not coercive, power.

persuasive power put to use to form a general consensus

Not surprisingly, some individuals in egalitarian societies are more skilled, imaginative, and successful negotiators than others, and their achievements do not go unrecognized. Indeed, their achievements lead other members of their society to accord them great prestige. Individuals in bands or tribes who enjoy such prestige may be asked for advice or deferred to when decisions must be made, because their past achievements, as hunters or ritual specialists, or fighters or diplomats, give their opinions greater weight than those of ordinary folk. Anthropologists have used the term **headman** to identify such individuals, who may be the ones chosen by their fellows to deal with outsiders in ambiguous or threatening situations. In fact, outsiders (such as representatives of a colonial power) often have assumed that members of indigenous groups who mediated between their own group and the colonial administration were leaders with coercive power. As we have seen, however, this assumption was incorrect when applied to headmen in bands or tribes, who have no capacity to force others to do their will. When colonial officials tried to incorporate "headmen" into their chain of command, expecting them to enforce compliance on the local level, they regularly discovered that, despite their prestige, headmen had no power to issue orders or force people to obey them. With the passage of time, under continued colonial rule, headmen often found themselves caught in an untenable position: expected by members of their own tribe to defend tribal interests against the colonial administration and expected by the colonial administration to extract compliance with colonial edicts from fellow tribesmen.

Another well-known anthropological example illustrating the exercise of persuasive power in egalitarian societies is that of the **big man.** Big men are "big" because of their ability to use their personal persuasive skills to arrange complex regional public events that involve kin and neighbors. In New Guinea, for example, big men gain personal prestige by organizing elaborate exchanges of valuables between their own and neighboring tribes. Such exchanges often begin as a kind of bloodwealth exchange: An end to hostilities is negotiated when the aggressors promise to present the aggrieved tribe with a quantity of wealth in the form of pigs, shells, money, and other valuables. Big men compete with one another to organize the collection and presentation of these goods, which is a major achievement, given that they have no coercive means to compel other members of their tribe to participate. Moreover, the initial exchange that marks the end of hostilities is rarely the last one. If the tribe that has received wealth wants to maintain or enhance its own prestige, it must eventually reciprocate with a return gift. It falls to big men in the receiving tribe to plan and carry out the reciprocal exchange, and they always aim to return more than they received, in order to enhance both their personal reputations and the reputation of their group. (+)

(+)   * *aim is to return more then they recieved*

7.7 Status and Role

The shift from egalitarian to stratified and from uncentralized to centralized political organization is also ordinarily a shift from largely informal sources of persuasive power to formally recognized social positions, or **statuses,** to which specific activities, or

roles, are attached (see other references in Chapter 6). Persons occupying formal political statuses in a state (e.g., tax collectors) need not rely purely on their personal persuasive ability to get others to do what they want. Instead, they possess **authority:** the ability to exert influence and even limited coercive power because they legitimately occupy a formal political office. The powers exercised by tax collectors are ordinarily strictly delimited; if they tried, say, to use the authority of their office to gain control of property to which they were not entitled, they probably would be punished. Still, as long as they stayed within their prescribed sphere, tax collectors would probably (if grudgingly) be recognized as within their rights to demand appropriate sums from properly identified citizens, and the citizens, more often than not, would comply.

7.8 Social Control and Law

State societies function successfully because all the complex activities that take place within them are monitored by a more or less complex army of hierarchically organized public functionaries, each occupying a separate formal office with its own proper responsibilities and coercive powers. This form of public administration, or **bureaucracy,** illustrates another distinctive feature of states as forms of political organization: the **formalization** of a wide range of tasks (see also Chapter 6). To formalize a bureaucratic or political office means to specify, explicitly and publicly, the rights and responsibilities of the officeholder. State societies formalize a wide range of tasks that are carried out by informal or barely formalized means in bands, tribes, and chiefdoms. For example, gossip is a very effective way to enforce conformity in small-scale societies without a police force. By contrast, state societies formalize not only leadership positions but also occupational qualifications and the public social rules that members of the society are expected to obey. Perhaps even more significantly, states formalize the **sanctions,** or penalties, to be meted out if social rules are broken.

Most anthropologists agree that, in societies without states, including chiefdoms, proper social conduct is enforced largely by local groups using informal means. When, however, a centralized government publicly sets forth both explicit formal definitions of right conduct and explicit penalties for failure to observe such standards and backs these definitions with its monopoly on coercive power, anthropologists generally agree that it is appropriate to speak of **law.** In particular, they have been interested in comparing the ways in which law has developed or is administered in noncapitalist state societies.

The appearance of formal law in a state does not mean that informal means of social control disappear. Rather, formal law is ordinarily used to sanction only the most serious crimes, such as theft, murder, or treason. Formal laws usually aim to be universal in scope, applying to all members of a society who possess certain attributes, and they usually focus on compliance (or lack thereof) with specific obligations (rights and duties) that all such individuals are expected to honor. Such a system of law is known as **substantive law,** and it is often the most interesting ethnographically, since it encodes notions of right conduct that show much cross-cultural variation. Substantive law contrasts with **procedural law,** which describes how those accused of breaking the law are to be treated. Anthropologists who compare legal systems cross-culturally also often distinguish between **civil law,** the breaking of which affects only one or a few individuals, and **criminal law,** which regulates attacks against society or the state. Modern industrial states have developed complex **law codes,** in which explicit rules covering many areas of social, economic, and political life are articulated, together with the penalties incurred for breaking them.

Of course, members of any society, when accused of breaking the law (informal or formal), often deny that they have done so. As we saw, egalitarian societies have developed their own informal ways of resolving such disputes, including mediation, feuding, and wealth exchange. In state societies, by contrast, formal laws and penalties are accompanied by formal legal institutions, such as **courts,** for resolving disputes. Informal dispute resolution remains in the hands of the affected parties: Recall that feuding kin groups, together with a mediator, must work out *a* resolution of their differences that satisfies the groups. Different disputants, however, might work out their differences in entirely different ways. It is this lack of uniformity in dispute resolution that a state tries to overcome in two ways. First, the state removes resolution of the dispute from the hands of the parties involved and puts it into the hands of a formal institution, the court; second, it evaluates the disputants' claims against the universal rights and responsibilities encoded in laws with uniform penalties. Because the court is supposed to be an impartial forum, care must be taken to ensure that the truth is told. Thus, all court systems develop rituals designed to achieve that end, such as the administration of oaths or ordeals to those who give evidence. In the end, the formal officers who preside in a court of law (i.e., judges) **adjudicate** the case before them; that is, based on the law code, they decide how a dispute will be settled.

Clearly, this entire apparatus can exist only in complex state societies producing sufficient surplus wealth to support the specialized formal court system, with its law code, lawyers, judges, and punishments. In other words, a formal system of laws requires a formal system of punishments, or penal code, without which a full-fledged court system cannot function. Indeed, this system defines, for the society in which it is found, what formally counts as **crime** and what does not. New laws can be promulgated that turn formerly tolerated behavior (e.g., public begging) into a crime or that decriminalize formerly illegal behavior (e.g., when taxes are abolished, not paying one's taxes is no longer illegal). Documenting changes in a legal system can offer important insights into the changing values and practices of the society to which the legal system belongs.

7.9 Nationalism and Hegemony

Much of the ethnographic data on which the previous discussions are based were gathered in societies that once enjoyed political autonomy but at some time in the last 500 years came under the economic or political control of Western colonial powers. To be sure, capitalist colonialism did not affect all areas of the world at the same time or to the same degree, and many precolonial political institutions and practices survived, albeit under changed circumstances, well into the twentieth century. But the last two decades of the twentieth century exhibited an intensified push of capitalist practices into those areas of the globe that previously had been buffered from some of their most disruptive effects. And many political anthropologists in recent years have become less interested in local political particularities and more interested in global forces that increasingly shape the opportunities for local political expression.

Such anthropologists pay attention to political processes that began with the spread of European colonial empires. Political conquest and incorporation within one or another European empire destroyed many indigenous political institutions. However, colonial political practices stimulated colonized peoples to rethink and rework their understanding of who they were and how they should do politics. Much current anthropological investigation focuses on the paradoxical consequences of political independence in former European colonies.

The issues are complex and varied, but many anthropologists have been interested in the phenomenon of **nationalism.** Traditionally, anthropologists used the term **nation** as a synonym for ethnic group or tribe—that is, to identify a social group whose members saw themselves as a single people, because of shared ancestry, culture, language, or history. Such nations/tribes/ethnic groups did not necessarily have any connection to political systems we call states until the late eighteenth century, and especially the nineteenth century, in Europe. By the end of the nineteenth century, many Europeans believed that the political boundaries of states should correspond with cultural and linguistic boundaries—that is, that states and nations should coincide and become **nation-states.** In the latter half of the twentieth century, newly independent postcolonial states tried to realize the nation-state ideal by attempting to build a shared sense of national identity among their citizens, most of whom belonged to groups that shared few or no political or cultural ties in precolonial times.

At the same time, many groups that claim a common "national" identity on the basis of culture or history or language find themselves encapsulated within a larger state or, worse, scattered across the territorial boundaries of more than one state. Following the nation-state logic, many of these groups see themselves as legitimate nations entitled to their own states. As the twenty-first century unfolds, the explosive potential built into these situations has created difficult political challenges for millions of people across the globe and seems to cry out for anthropological analysis.

Many anthropologists have borrowed Benedict Anderson's concept of the nation as an **imagined community** (also discussed in Chapter 2), whose members' knowledge of one another does not come from regular face-to-face interactions but instead is based on their shared experiences with national institutions, such as schools or government bureaucracies, and the bonds created from reading the same newspapers and books. The often violent postcolonial histories of aspiring nation-states, involving coups d'état and civil strife, has demonstrated to participants and observers alike that national identity cannot be imposed by coercion alone. Persuasive power must also be used, which is why anthropologists have drawn on the work of Antonio Gramsci (1891–1937). Reflecting on the reasons the Italian nation-state was so much less successful in becoming unified than its European neighbors, Gramsci emphasized a contrast between the role of authoritarian domination (or coercive power) and hegemony (or persuasive power) that many contemporary social scientists have found useful. **Domination** can put a regime in power, but domination alone will not keep it in power. For one thing, it is expensive to keep soldiers and police on constant alert against resistance; for another, the people come to resent continued military surveillance, which turns them against the regime. This is why long-term stability requires rulers to use persuasive means to win the support of their subjects, thereby making a constant public show of force unnecessary. Gramsci used the term **hegemony** to describe control achieved by such persuasive means.

A variety of tactics can be used to build hegemony, including neutralizing opposition from powerful groups by granting them special privileges, and articulating an explicit **ideology** that explains the rulers' right to rule and justifies inequality. If the ideology is widely promulgated throughout the society (e.g., in schools, through media) and if rulers make occasional public gestures that benefit large sections of the population, they may forestall rebellion and even win the loyalty of those whom they dominate. Because hegemony depends on persuasive power, however, it is vulnerable to the critical attention of the powerless, whose reflections on their own experiences may lead them to question the ruling ideology. They may even develop interpretations of their political situation that challenge the official ideology. Sometimes the term **hidden transcripts** is used to describe these alternative (or *counterhegemonic*) understandings, since they are frequently too dangerous to be openly proclaimed. Because hidden transcripts offer an alternative, however, they offer openings to more sustained critiques of the status quo that eventually could lead to open rebellion.

Many anthropologists find the concept of hegemony to be useful because it offers a way of showing that oppressed groups that do not rise up in open revolt against their oppressors have *not* necessarily been brainwashed by the hegemonic ideology. Rather, such groups possess sufficient agency to create counterhegemonic interpretations of their own oppression. If they do not take up arms, therefore, this is probably because they have accurately concluded that rebellion would not succeed under current conditions. The concepts of hegemony and hidden transcripts help anthropologists to demonstrate that political concepts such as "freedom," "justice," and "democracy" do not have fixed meanings but may be the focus of cultural and political struggle between powerful and powerless groups in a society.

7.10 Summary

In this chapter, we discussed several ways in which anthropologists analyze power. We looked at coercive power, including warfare, and at persuasive power. We examined societies with different kinds of political hierarchies. And we considered the distinct ways in which anthropologists understand law and outlined the features of nationalism and hegemony.

For Further Reading

POWER
Arens and Karp 1989; Wolf 1999

POLITICAL ANTHROPOLOGY
Fried 1967; Lewellen 1992; Service 1962, 1975

LAW
Harris 1997; Nader 1997; Pospisil 1971

NATIONALISM
Anderson 1983; Hughey 1998; Tambiah 1997

HEGEMONY AND HIDDEN TRANSCRIPTS
Scott 1987, 1992

8

Economic Anthropology

The key terms and concepts covered in this chapter, in the order in which they appear:

domestic groups

subsistence strategies
domestication
foragers
food producers
transhumance
slash-and-burn
swidden
shifting cultivation
extensive agriculture
intensive agriculture
mechanized industrial
   agriculture
surpluses

capitalism

formalists

economy

scarcity

substantivists
original affluent society
modes of exchange
reciprocity
redistribution
potlatch
leveling mechanisms

proletariat
bourgeoisie

labor
means of production
consumers
alienation
mode of production
classes
relations of production

peasant
cash crops
production for use
production for exchange

formal economy
informal economy
articulating modes of
   production

consumption
basic human needs

ecological
   anthropologists
human ecologists
behavioral ecological
   anthropologists
culture inheritance
   theorists

conspicuous
   consumption

SINCE ITS FORMATIVE YEARS as a discipline, anthropology has been interested in the many and varied ways in which human beings in different societies make a living. In the late nineteenth century, anthropologists devoted much attention to the tools and techniques developed by various peoples to secure their material survival and well-being in a range of climates and habitats. Indeed, the objects people made for these purposes—spears, snares, fishnets, bows, arrows, hoes, plows, baskets, and the like —formed the collections of early ethnological museums in Europe and North America. Early anthropological theorists paid particular attention to the activities in which these objects figured, called the "arts of subsistence" by Lewis Henry Morgan (1818–81).

8.1 The "Arts of Subsistence"

Morgan focused on large-scale variation in patterns of the arts of subsistence in different human societies when he constructed his great unilineal scheme of cultural evolution (a discussion of this approach is found in Chapter 12). His key criterion for ranking subsistence patterns was technological complexity: the simpler the toolkit, the more "primitive" the society's arts of subsistence. Morgan's final scheme encompassed three great "ethnical periods"—Savagery, Barbarism, and Civilization—through which, he claimed, every human society either had passed or would pass as it evolved.

Morgan assumed that the society in which he lived had evolved further and faster than others on the globe and that, consequently, the arts of subsistence characteristic of those other societies could accurately be described in terms not only of what they possessed but also of what they lacked. Thus, "savages" were all those peoples who had never domesticated plants or animals for their subsistence. Morgan subdivided them into lower, middle, and upper categories based on the complexity of the tools and skills they had devised for living off nature's bounty; "upper savages," for example, not only controlled fire and fished but had mastered the bow and arrow. The invention of pottery signaled for them the beginning of Barbarism. "Barbarians" herded animals and/or cultivated plants, and they also invented new subsistence tools and techniques, such as iron implements and irrigated fields. All these advances were incorporated into the next ethnical period, that of "Civilization," which Morgan believed could be identified as soon as writing appeared.

Anthropologists have long since removed terms like *savage* and *barbarian* from their professional analytic vocabulary. They are well aware of how evolutionary schemes like Morgan's can be (and have been) used to rationalize the domination of the world by so-called civilized societies. But one does not have to accept these aspects of Morgan's analysis to recognize the importance of his classification of different arts of subsistence. He had collected information about a wide range of societies. He had hypothesized that variation in their arts of subsistence was systematic, showing up, for example, in correlations between particular technological developments and particular forms of social organization (especially kinship organization) in **domestic groups** (i.e., those whose members live in the same household). Karl Marx and Friedrich Engels (1820–95) read Morgan and were persuaded that his ethnical periods documented changes in precapitalist modes of production. But again, one does not have to be a Marxist to be both impressed and puzzled by the patterns of subsistence to which Morgan drew attention.

8.2 Subsistence Strategies

In early-twentieth-century North America, Franz Boas and his students, having roundly rejected unilineal schemes of cultural evolution, were suspicious of grand explanations and unwilling to make far-reaching claims (for more on the Boasians, see Chapter 12). But they were interested in documenting with great care how particular peoples went about making their living. As a result, throughout much of the first half of the twentieth century, anthropologists hesitated to do more than offer a loose categorization of the various subsistence strategies adopted by the peoples of the earth. The **subsistence strategies** identified—hunting and gathering (foraging), pastoralism, horticulture, and agriculture—reiterated the distinctions that Morgan had recognized.

The key feature distinguishing these strategies is **domestication:** regular human interference with the reproduction of other species in ways that makes them beneficial to ourselves. Hunter-gatherers—now usually called **foragers** or food collectors—are those who do not rely on domesticated plants or animals but instead subsist on a variety of wild foodstuffs. Their knowledge of their habitats is encyclopedic, and they manage to live quite well by roaming over large tracts of land in search of particular seasonal plant foods, water sources, or game. By contrast, practitioners of the other three subsistence strategies depend on domesticated species and so are sometimes referred to as **food producers** rather than food collectors. Pastoralists rely on herds of domesticated animals, such as cattle, camels, sheep, or goats, and regularly move these herds, sometimes over great distances, as water and forage in one area are used up. In many parts of the world, these movements are patterned in yearly cycles of **transhumance,** as herders move from dry-season pastures to wet-season pastures and back again.

Horticulturalists cultivate domesticated plants by using human labor and simple tools and techniques to modify local vegetation or soil texture before planting their crops. In **slash-and-burn** or **swidden** cultivation, for example, hand tools are used to cut down all vegetation except large trees from an area to be planted. The vegetation is then burned, and the ash serves to fertilize the crops. But swidden farmers can use a particular field for only a few growing seasons before the soil is exhausted and must be left fallow for several years to regenerate. As a result, swidden farmers must move on to clear new fields every few years, which is why their practices are sometimes also referred to as **shifting cultivation.** Shifting cultivation is highly productive and energy efficient, but it functions well only when farmers have access to enough

---

TABLE 8.1   Major Subsistence Strategies

Foraging
Herding
Extensive agriculture (also known as horticulture, slash-and-burn, swidden)
Intensive agriculture
Industrialized food production

---

land to live on while old fields lie fallow long enough (often from seven to ten years) to regenerate. Shifting cultivation is thus sometimes also called **extensive agriculture** because so much land is required to support so few people.

Only with **intensive agriculture** do we find societies exploiting the strength of domestic animals, by harnessing them to more complex tools like plows and growing and harvesting crops with the help of irrigation and fertilizers. Intensive agriculturalists first appeared some 10,000 years ago in Southwest Asia. Their farming practices are intensive because the techniques they employ allow them to produce more than shifting cultivators could produce on the same amount of land, while keeping their fields in continuous use. Contemporary intensive farming practices, often called **mechanized industrial agriculture,** rely on industrial technology for machinery, fertilizers, pesticides, and herbicides. This form of agriculture uses vastly more energy than does shifting cultivation, but it enables a few farmers to produce enormous amounts of food on vast expanses of land, their "factories in the field." (Table 8.1 lists the major subsistence strategies.)

Intensive agriculture marked an important break from forms of extensive agriculture because it allowed farmers to produce **surpluses** beyond what they required to survive from harvest to harvest and still save enough seed for the next year's crop. Agricultural surpluses supported the first ancient civilizations by making possible new and complex forms of social organization, involving a specialized division of labor that promoted technical

developments in all areas of material life. Writing and its analogues (such as the *quipu* in Andean civilizations) did not drive
these changes, but they were extremely useful for various kinds of
political, economic, and social record-keeping.

8.3 Explaining the Material Life Processes of Society

In general, fieldworking cultural anthropologists have left investigation of the origin of subsistence strategies and the rise of ancient
civilizations to archaeologists and prehistorians. Given the pernicious use to which extreme and exaggerated unilineal evolutionary claims had been put in the nineteenth century, early-twentieth-
century ethnographers preferred to document the enormous
amount of diversity still to be found in the material life of living
societies. But this pursuit of cultural documentation, apparently
for its own sake, struck later generations of anthropologists as
unwarranted and pernicious in its own way. They sensed there
were patterns to be detected and explained, and this required a
professional willingness to develop theories that could generalize
across particular cases.

One attempt to reintroduce theory into the anthropological
study of material life was made by Melville Herskovits (1895–
1963) around the time of World War II. Herskovits urged anthropologists to borrow concepts and theories from neoclassical economics, the scholarly discipline rooted in Adam Smith's efforts in
the eighteenth century to make sense of the new Western economic
system later known as **capitalism.** Herskovits was persuaded that
the concepts and theories of neoclassical economies had been
refined to such a degree of scientific objectivity and formal preci-
sion that they could be applied to economies very different from
the one they originally were invented to explain. Those anthropologists who decided to follow Herskovits's suggestion came to be
known as formal economic anthropologists, or **formalists.**

Formalists took concepts like *supply, demand, price,* and
money, which had successfully been used to analyze economic
activity in capitalist market economies, and searched for their

analogues in non-Western, noncapitalist societies. They realized, of course, that many such societies had no system of coinage performing all the functions Western money performed. But they noted that objects like iron bars or lengths of cloth or shells often seemed to be used much the way people in capitalist societies used money, as a medium of exchange or measure of value. And so formalists tried to use the ideas neoclassical economists had developed about money to make sense of, say, the way people in society X used shells. Or formalists might analyze customs in which a groom's family offered material valuables to the family of a bride to solemnize a marriage. This transaction looked very much like a "purchase," with something other than money being offered in exchange for a highly valued "good," the bride. Formalists thus tried to explain how much it "cost" to "pay for" a bride in the society. Adopting the assumptions of neoclassical theory, formalists assumed that each party to a marriage transaction would try to get as much as possible out of the transaction while giving as little as possible in return. Therefore, the number of cattle actually accepted in exchange for a bride would be subject to the forces of supply and demand, and the parties would agree on a "bride price" whereby supply and demand balanced.

Formalists did not view themselves as ethnocentric when they analyzed non-Western, noncapitalist economic activities in this way. They thought that any culture-bound features of the concepts and theories they were using had long since been eliminated. But other anthropologists disagreed. These critics believed that, despite its sophistication, neoclassical economic theory still bore many traces of its origins in Western capitalist society. Perhaps the most obvious trace could be seen in the neoclassical understanding of just what **economy** meant: buying cheap and selling dear in order to maximize one's individual utility (or satisfaction).

Critics pointed out that neoclassical economics, like capitalist society itself, subscribes to a particular view of human nature that sees isolated individuals as the only genuine human reality. That is, human beings are viewed as creatures who are by nature self-interested egoists who always act in ways that will increase their own individual well-being. Moreover, human beings all live under conditions of **scarcity**; that is, there will never be enough of all the material goods they desire to go around. As a result, the basic human condition consists of isolated individuals competing with one another, under conditions of scarcity, to obtain as much of what they want for as little as possible. Society might view such behavior negatively as selfish or greedy, but according to the neo-classical view, human society is artificial, secondary, and legitimate only to the extent that social rules do not interfere with each individual's pursuit of his or her own self-interest. That is, in a world of isolated individuals competing for access to scarce goods, looking out for Number One turns out to be a good thing —indeed, the *rational* thing to do—because putting others' needs first might interfere with maximizing one's own happiness.

Still, Adam Smith and others believed that when competition was carried out among individuals of more or less equal wealth and power, private vice could lead to public virtue. For instance, if you tried to cheat your customers, word would get around, and they would buy from other producers, causing you to lose money. Thus, you end up happier if you make your customers happy as well. Indeed, the price on which the two of you decide ideally ought to provide the best possible value either party might hope to obtain.

Only if such a view of human nature is accepted does neoclassical economic theory make sense. But anthropological critics were convinced that such a view of universal "human nature" could *not* make sense of the economic practices ethnographers had discovered in the *particular* non-Western, noncapitalist societies where they had done fieldwork. They pointed out that many non-Western economic systems were built on the assumption that human beings were, first and foremost, social creatures with legitimate obligations to other members of the societies in which they lived. Indeed, economic arrangements in such societies were shaped to the contours of other religious or political or kinship institutions in the society. That is, economic activities were *embedded* in the noneconomic institutions that made the society as a whole function properly. Rather than a measure of how individuals universally allocated scarce resources among alternative (presumably universal) ends, these anthropologists preferred to think of an economy as the concrete (and particular) way in which material goods and services were made available to members of a given society. Capitalism might allow individuals the freedom to pursue their own self-interest apart from the interests of others, but such an economic system was a recent and unusual addition to the ethnographic and historical record. Those anthropologists who defined economic systems in terms of their substantive institutional arrangements for provisioning their members came to be called **substantivists.** Substantivists argued that describing noncapitalist economic systems using neoclassical economic theory could only distort and misrepresent what was actually going on in those economies.

American anthropologist Marshall Sahlins, a leading substantivist, set about debunking what he viewed as formalist misrepresentation of economic life in non-Western, noncapitalist societies. After surveying a substantial ethnographic literature that described how foragers made a living, for example, Sahlins asked Westerners to reconsider how people might come to obtain more than enough of whatever they wanted—that is, become "affluent." Since the rise of industrial capitalism, many people assumed that the only path to affluence was by producing much, but Sahlins argued that a second "Zen road" to affluence consisted in desiring little. Foragers had very few material desires, and the habitats in which they lived were more than able to satisfy these needs. Thus, Sahlins concluded, the **original affluent society** was not industrial capitalism, but foraging.

8.4 Modes of Exchange

Sahlins also drew upon the work of economic historian Karl Polanyi, whose work also showed just how misleading it was to suppose that all human economies, in all times and places, had been based on capitalist principles, given that the key components of market capitalism had come together only within the past few centuries in western Europe. Polanyi distinguished among different **modes of exchange**—the patterns according to which distribution takes place—and argued that the capitalist mode of market

TABLE 8.2   Modes of Exchange

Reciprocity
    Generalized
    Balanced
    Negative
Redistribution
Market exchange

exchange followed principles quite different from the principles that governed exchange in pre- or noncapitalist societies. He emphasized two particular noncapitalist modes of exchange: reciprocity and redistribution.

Sahlins borrowed Polanyi's classification of modes of exchange and tested them against a wide range of ethnographic data. He found that **reciprocity** governed exchange in small, face-to-face societies, especially those whose members lived by foraging. He also distinguished different forms of reciprocity. *Generalized* reciprocity involved no record-keeping, and parties assumed that exchanges would balance out in the long run. *Balanced* reciprocity required both that a gift be repaid within a set time limit and that goods exchanged be of roughly the same value. *Negative* reciprocity involved parties who repeatedly tried to get something for nothing from one another in a relationship that might continue over time, each trying to get the better of the other.

Redistribution as a mode of exchange requires the presence in a society of some central person or institution. Goods flow toward this central point and are then redistributed among members of the society according to their cultural norms of what is appropriate. (Table 8.2 lists the basic modes of exchange.) Varieties of redistribution range from such non-Western institutions as the **potlatch** practiced by the indigenous inhabitants of the northwest coast of North America to the income tax and social welfare institutions of modern nation-states. To the degree that they exist, modes of redistribution act as **leveling mechanisms;** that is, they shrink gaps between rich and poor. In noncapitalist societies integrated by redistribution, the person responsible for amassing and then redistributing goods earned great prestige for his generosity, but he was often materially worse off afterward than most other members of the group. Polanyi pointed out that both reciprocity and redistribution may persist in societies organized along capitalist lines. In the United States, for example, exchange relations between parents and children ordinarily are governed by generalized reciprocity, and the collection of income taxes and the dispersal of government subsidies to citizens involves redistribution; but most goods and services are produced and exchanged by means of capitalist market mechanisms.

Similar ideas were developed by French anthropologist Marcel Mauss (1872–1950), one of Emile Durkheim's colleagues, who contrasted *gift* economies of small-scale non-Western societies (based on reciprocity and laden with culturally significant noncommercial values) with *commodity* exchanges (in which a good's value is mediated by the capitalist market). A number of contemporary European anthropologists have developed Mauss's ideas to mount their own critique of market-centered analyses of noncapitalist economies.

8.5 Production, Distribution, and Consumption

The debate between the formalists and the substantivists about the proper way to do economic anthropology became quite bitter in the late 1950s and early 1960s, with no resolution. Hindsight reveals that the divide between them was sharpened by the Cold War. In the Cold War years (which stretched from the late 1940s to 1989, when the Soviet Union broke apart), the ideological opposition between the Western "free market" (the First World) and Soviet "communism" (the Second World) was so strong that anyone in the United States who questioned neoclassical economic theory ran the risk of being labeled a "communist sympathizer," which was virtually synonymous with "traitor." Especially after the Cuban Communist Revolution in 1959, views of economic life in non-Western societies that validated the assumptions of neoclassical theory were encouraged by members of the political elite in the United States. They hoped that, by showing a free-market route to economic prosperity, they could keep nations newly freed from colonial control (soon to be known as the Third World) from following Cuba's example.

But the late 1960s and 1970s brought a new dynamic to the Cold War. Citizens in Western countries began to question publicly the official Cold War rhetoric they had been taught. In those unsettled years, some economic anthropologists began to study texts by Marx and his followers. Marxian economic analysis, which offered its own set of formal concepts and theories, appealed to these anthropologists, and they tried to use Marxian analysis to make sense of their ethnographic data on non-Western economic life.

Although the debates among economic anthropologists can sometimes still become bitter, dialogue remains viable because all of them, regardless of perspective, largely agree that economic life can be divided into three phases: production, distribution, and consumption. Where they disagree concerns what motivates human beings to engage in economic activity in the first place and which (if any) of the three phases of economic life is the most important in any economic system. Neoclassical economic theorists, dazzled by the power of modern capitalist markets, saw *distribution* to be key. After all, prices are set in the market when suppliers of goods and buyers of goods reach agreement about how much to offer for what. Historically, capitalist markets developed under circumstances in late-medieval European cities in which certain kinds of people—merchants, artisans—engaged in economic transactions free of the feudal obligations that controlled exchange between lords and peasants in rural areas. This freedom from obligations to others—the freedom to take one's chances buying and selling in the market—seemed to validate a view of human nature that eventually justified neoclassical economic theory in a society in which capitalism had triumphed. And it was a theory written primarily from the point of view of those who had engaged in free-market transactions and prospered.

Marx and his followers, however, paid attention to those whose participation in free capitalist markets kept them mired in poverty. These were the **proletariat,** the workers who toiled for wages in factories owned by the **bourgeoisie,** capitalists who sold for profit the commodities the workers produced. The very different positions of capitalists and workers was due to the fact that capitalists owned or controlled the means of production, whereas the workers owned nothing but their own labor power, which they were forced to sell to the capitalist at whatever price he was willing to pay, in order to survive. The transformation of once communally shared, productive property into the private property of individuals was viewed by Marx as the historical change that, together with industrial technology, produced the capitalist mode of production. The unequal relationship between workers and owners under capitalism meant that, when both met in the market to buy and sell, some of them (the capitalist owners) had considerably greater economic power than did others (the workers). The origins of that inequality required that attention be paid to the *production* phase of economic life.

Although not sentimental about precapitalist economic relations, Marxists pointed out that the "freedom" of free enterprise is double-edged. Noncapitalist economic relations were regularly hedged about with rights and obligations, as the substantivists and Mauss had stressed, and while these certainly constrained the ability of any individual to put his own selfish needs first, they also protected individuals from destitution. Even feudal peasants had economic rights their lords were obliged to respect. But both the protections and the constraints disappeared once labor became "free" in a capitalist system.

Labor is a central concept for a Marxian analysis of economic production, especially social labor in which people work together to transform the material world into forms they can use. In noncapitalist economic systems, people ordinarily work with others to produce goods for their own use, using tools and materials that belong to them. Under industrial capitalism, all this changes. For example, workers might produce shoes in a factory, but shoes, along with the tools, technology, and materials used to make them —what Marx called the **means of production**—belong to the factory owner, not to the workers. Instead, workers receive money wages in exchange for their labor. With these wages, they are supposed to purchase in the market food, clothing, and other goods to meet their subsistence needs; that is, they become **consumers.** Because workers compete with one another for scarce wage work, they must put their individual self-interest first if they are to survive; thus, they come to view their fellows as rivals rather than comrades.

In all these ways, Marx argued, life under capitalism separates workers from the means of production, from the goods they produce, and from other human beings, a situation he called **alienation.** For Marxists, therefore, the isolated individual who is the hero of the capitalist version of "human nature" is actually an alienated social being forced into existence under the historically recent economic conditions of Western capitalism. Marx and most of his followers were interested in understanding how these socioeconomic conditions had developed in Western European societies. Like Marx, many also found the situation intolerable and believed that the point was not to understand society but to change it.

Marxian ideas exerted a powerful influence in anthropology in the latter third of the twentieth century, and economic anthropologists have drawn from them in a variety of ways. It is important to emphasize, however, that even those anthropologists with strong commitments to leftist politics feel quite free to criticize and to reject specific Marxian assumptions or concepts as they see fit. Among those Marxian concepts that have been the most important in economic anthropology, we will emphasize here only one: the mode of production.

8.6 Mode of Production

Marx characterized European capitalism as a mode of production, and he contrasted it with the feudal mode of production that preceded it. A **mode of production** refers generally to the way the production of material goods in a society is carried out. Not only does it involve the tools, knowledge, and skills needed for production (i.e., the means of production), but it also depends on a particular division of social labor in terms of which different groups, or **classes,** of people are responsible for various productive activities, or the **relations of production.** In the feudal and capitalist modes of production, the central division of labor was between rulers and ruled: lords and peasants in feudalism, and owners and workers in capitalism.

A key element in the Marxian analysis of modes of production concerns the nature of the relationship linking classes to one another in a particular society. Marx's point was that, although both classes had to work together for production to succeed, their economic interests were nevertheless contradictory because of their different relations to the means of production. For example, workers want the profits from their labor to go into higher wages, whereas the owners would prefer to keep wages low and keep as much profit as they can for themselves. The potential for class conflict was therefore built into any mode of production. Eventually, Marx predicted, these class contradictions would undermine the mode of production, leading to a revolution that would bring forth a new and improved mode of production.

Anthropologists studying economic conditions in different societies do not necessarily accept Marx's prophecies about revolution. But they have wondered whether the noncapitalist economic patterns revealed by fieldwork might usefully be understood as different modes of production. Some anthropologists working in Africa, for example, thought that the economic arrangements they observed among people who organized their societies (and their economic activities) on the basis of kinship might be framed as a *lineage mode of production*. That is, the opposed "classes" were elder and younger groups within particular lineages that owned important economic resources like agricultural land and implements (the *means* or *forces of production*). Like owners and workers under capitalism, the economic interests of elders and juniors were opposed and might lead to conflict: elders wanted to maintain their control over the forces of production, while juniors wanted to take it away.

8.7 Peasants

Other anthropologists have talked about a *peasant mode of production* observable in many contemporary Latin American societies. These societies are seen to be divided into classes, with peasants dominated by a ruling class of landowners and merchants. Anthropologists use the word **peasant** to refer to small-scale farmers in state societies who own their own means of production (simple tools, seed, and so forth) and who produce enough to feed themselves and to pay rent to their landlords and taxes to the government. Anthropologists have wondered how much autonomy peasants might have in particular societies and under what circumstances that autonomy might be undermined by changing political and economic conditions. For example, what happens to peasants who are forced to deal with the increasing penetration of capitalist market relations?

Many of the world's peasants were first introduced to capitalism as a result of European colonization. Colonized peasants continued to grow subsistence crops for their own consumption, but European colonizers regularly encouraged them to grow other crops that they could sell for cash. Sometimes these **cash crops** had been produced traditionally; in northern Cameroon in Africa, for example, peanuts were a traditional crop that local farmers began to sell on the market during the colonial period. Other times, cash crops were introduced from outside; in northern Cameroon, French colonial authorities introduced the variety of cotton now grown by local farmers and sold for cash. In this way, peasant **production for use** was pushed by colonial authorities in the direction of capitalist **production for exchange** in the capitalist market.

This form of agriculture (i.e., producing crops to be sold for cash rather than to be consumed at home) has had far-reaching effects on the economic life of peasants. To begin with, peasant farmers could continue to produce much of what they consumed, using the money they received for their cash crops to purchase imported goods or to pay taxes and school fees. Unfortunately, by using some of their land to plant cash crops, less was left to plant subsistence crops. In many cases, this led over time to increasing dependence on the money from cash cropping to buy necessities that could no longer be produced, or produced in sufficient quantity, to keep a peasant household going. Indeed, many ethnographers have documented situations in which members of ostensibly "peasant" households regularly leave the farm to perform wage work on plantations or in factories. Without this additional income, many peasant households would collapse.

And this situation, in which members of the same household are alternately farmers and wage workers, has led anthropologists to wonder exactly how to describe and analyze what they are seeing. Are these peasants no longer truly peasants? Does their increasing reliance on wage work for survival mean that they have been "captured" by an expanding capitalist mode of production? Have they been transformed from peasants into a rural proletariat? Some anthropologists have argued that this is indeed the case, and some ethnographic materials support their arguments. In other cases, however, the situation is more complicated. Although members of peasant households rely on wage work to keep their families going, they continue to farm, producing much of the food needed for household subsistence. Some anthropologists refer to these peasants-who-are-also-wage-workers as members of an emerging *peasantariat*.

From the perspective of neoclassical economic theory, members of this Third World peasantariat were understood to be "in transition" from "traditional" to "modern" (i.e., capitalist) economic practices. Neoclassical theory argued that capitalist economic institutions (those that paid taxes, obeyed government regulations, and otherwise adhered to rules set down by the state) belonged to sectors of the modern, national, **formal economy,** into which other, so-called backward sectors of the **informal economy** eventually would be absorbed. In former colonies that had recently become independent states, the formal sector was often quite small, whereas the informal economy was very important, especially in urban areas. Many migrants supported themselves and their families by engaging in all sorts of unregulated, untaxed, and even illegal economic activities, from smuggling, to peddling, to selling cooked food. They also might move from a period of employment within the formal sector to a period in the informal sector and then back again. Moreover, anthropological fieldwork showed that many people active in the formal or informal economy of a city might also have ties to relatives in rural areas who engaged in agriculture and with whom they pooled economic resources.

TABLE 8.3 Modes of Production
Kin-ordered
Tributary
Capitalist
Articulating

Anthropologists working in many so-called Third World societies documented the seeming resilience of precapitalist economic arrangements confronted by more recent capitalist institutions. Such arrangements seemed to be delaying indefinitely the promised transition from "tradition" to capitalist "modernity." Anthropologists of a neoclassical bent might argue that the transition was still inevitable but would simply take longer than they originally predicted. But others of a Marxian bent might suggest that the situation could be best described as a social formation composed of two or more **articulating modes of production.** That is, in settings such as former European colonies in Africa, precapitalist modes of production and the capitalist mode of production, each organized according to different relations of production, apparently have adapted to each other's presence. Under such circumstances, individuals and groups could participate in the precolonial relations of production when participation in the capitalist relations of production was too costly or did not suit them for other reasons. Some anthropologists have argued that, in this way, people were able to defend themselves against the potentially destructive effects of the capitalist market. (Table 8.3 lists some basic modes of production.)

8.8 Consumption

The final phase of economic activity is **consumption,** when the goods or services produced in a society are distributed to those who use them up, or consume them. Most economists, whether of neoclassical or Marxian persuasion, traditionally have had little to say about why it is that *these* goods and *these* services (as opposed to other goods and services) get produced and distributed. Either consumption preferences are reduced to the idiosyncratic, unpredictable, and inexplicable choices of individuals (as in neoclassical economics), or they are reduced to basic biological needs (as when Marx stated that human beings need first to eat and drink before they can make history). Some anthropologists have made similar arguments. Bronislaw Malinowski, for example, wanted to show that "primitive" peoples were, in fact, no less human than their "civilized" counterparts. He argued that, although all viable societies must satisfy their members' universal **basic human needs** for food, shelter, companionship, and so forth, each society has invented its own cultural way of meeting those needs. Malinowski's approach, however, failed to address the question of *why,* for example, Trobriand Islanders satisfied their need for food with yams and pork rather than with, say, sorghum and beef.

One way to answer such a question is to point out that yams and pork are locally available for consumption in the ecological setting to which Trobriand Islanders have become adapted. Answers of this form to questions about consumption were developed by ecological anthropologists beginning in the 1950s. **Ecological anthropologists** seek to understand a particular human group as but one population of living things, coexisting with other living populations in a particular environment. They share the same focus as other scholars who call themselves **human ecologists.** The approach of ecological anthropologists differs somewhat from that of other ecologists interested in humans, primarily because anthropologists have always been interested in how human dependence on culture mediates human adaptation to the environment. In any case, ecologically oriented anthropologists also disagree with one another about the importance of culture in human evolution and ecological adaptation. **Behavioral ecological anthropologists,** for example, have been heavily influenced by the ideas of sociobiology, a school of evolutionary thought that assigns culture little or no role in human adaptation but instead argues that genetically driven and/or environmentally driven necessity keep(s) culture "on a short leash." Other anthropologists, such as

> **TABLE 8.4   Approaches to Consumption**
>
> Basic human needs (Malinowski)
> Ecological
>   Behavioral ecological anthropology
>   Cultural ecology/cultural inheritance theory
> Cultural/arbitrary

culture inheritance theorists, find sociobiological accounts inadequate. They argue that symbolic culture has played a key mediating role in human evolution and that it continues to exert powerful influences on contemporary human ecological adaptations. (Table 8.4 lists some basic approaches to consumption.)

Culture appears to play an important role in consumption patterns for at least two reasons. First, consumption preferences often are more closely linked to membership in particular social groups than to the ecological setting in which one lives. Second, the consumption preferences people share often involve goods and services that are not easily explained with reference to basic human biological needs. A good illustration is the pattern found in capitalist societies that sociologist and economist Thorstein Veblen (1857–1929) labeled conspicuous consumption. **Conspicuous consumption** involves the purchase and public display of goods known to be costly and unnecessary for basic survival. For example, many people who live in the suburban United States find it necessary to own an automobile for transportation. Getting from home to work to the supermarket to the shopping mall in no way requires the extra speed and power of a sports car, but many suburban residents nevertheless spend tens of thousands of dollars for sports cars. Veblen suggested, and cultural anthropologists agree, that people who drive these cars do so more for symbolic than for practical reasons. That is, they want to show other people (especially those whom they want to impress) that they are so prosperous that they are not limited to purchasing goods for purely practical reasons; rather, they can "waste" cash on non-necessities, on luxurious, ostentatious extras.

Even though our continued existence requires a minimal level of food, water, shelter, and human companionship, ethnographic research has powerfully demonstrated that it is virtually impossible to separate peoples' indispensable *needs* from their discretionary *wants*. This is because all human groups attach cultural meanings to the goods and services they consume. For this reason, Veblen's pattern of conspicuous consumption within the capitalist mode of production constitutes only one end of the continuum of consumption practices documented for different societies with different modes of production. In all cases, what people consume makes a statement about who they are, what they value, and where their loyalties lie.

The anthropological study of consumption has contributed greatly to a critique of approaches to consumption that would reduce it to biological necessity or individual idiosyncrasy. Anthropologists have shown how consumption patterns associated with such seemingly unproblematic foods as meat or sugar have been shaped by cultural beliefs and practices in different times and places. In particular, they have shown what happens when consumption goods are turned into commodities under a capitalist mode of production. This process has been under way now for several centuries and continues to affect the consumption choices of people throughout the world. For example, "fast food" becomes highly valued when a capitalist mode of production draws into the paid workforce those household members who previously had the time, energy, and resources to prepare meals from scratch. And the particular kind of fast food people come to prefer increasingly is shaped by expensive media campaigns designed to persuade consumers using the same tactics Veblen described a century ago.

Many anthropologists have begun to examine the way consumption practices in non-Western societies are changing as a result of these processes, however, and they have been able to show that non-Western consumers of Western-made products are not simply the dupes of advertisers and marketers. Rather, the members of many societies in the world have selected some Western material goods and rejected others based on how well they think those goods will enhance or enrich their own traditions. Thus, Otavalan weavers purchase television sets to entertain weavers producing traditional textiles in locally owned shops, with the result that production increases, enabling Otavalan merchants to more successfully compete in an international market for indigenous products. Under such circumstances, the consumption of television strengthens, rather than diminishes, Otavalan tradition. Indeed, the recent successful participation in the institutions of international capitalism by non-Western peoples, from Otavalan textile producers to Japanese, Chinese, and Korean businessmen, suggests that there is perhaps nothing intrinsically "western" about capitalism. These cases suggest that consumption of goods sold in capitalist markets need not mean that consumers are being obediently programmed to replace their own traditions with Western consumerism; instead, they are *indigenizing* and *domesticating* capitalist practices and consumer goods as they create their own alternative versions of modernity.

8.9 Summary

In this chapter, we looked at the range of subsistence strategies that different kinds of societies have employed. We also considered two different theoretical approaches taken by anthropologists in analyzing economic activity—the formalist and the substantivist. And we have looked at exchange approaches, production approaches, and different consumption approaches to economic activity.

For Further Reading

ECONOMIC ANTHROPOLOGY

Gudeman 1986; Halperin 1994; Littlefield and Gates 1991; Plattner 1989; Sahlins 1972; Wilk 1996

PEASANTS

Kearney 1996; Netting 1993; Wolf 1962, 1982

CONSUMPTION

Coe and Coe 1996; Colloredo-Mansfeld 1999; Fiddis 1991; Mintz 1985, 1996

MONEY

Weatherford 1997

9

Kinship and Descent

The key terms and concepts covered in this chapter, in the order in which they appear:

kinship
new reproductive
   technologies
descent
consanguineal kin
adoption

bilateral descent
cognatic descent
bilateral kindred

unilineal descent
patrilineal
agnatic

matrilineal
uterine
unilineal descent
   groups
patrilineage
matrilineage
lineage
clan

kinship terminologies
fictive kin
generation
gender
affinity

collaterality
bifurcation
relative age
sex of linking relative
parallel cousins
cross cousins

Hawaiian
Eskimo
Iroquois
bifurcate merging
Crow
Omaha
Sudanese

From the birth of their discipline in the late nineteenth century, anthropologists have been interested in **kinship:** the various systems of social organization that societies have constructed on principles derived from the universal human experiences of mating, birth, and nurturance. Members of Western societies influenced by the sciences of biology and genetics frequently believe that kinship relationships are (or should be) a direct reflection of the biology and genetics of human reproduction. Nevertheless, they are aware that, even in their own societies, kinship is not the same thing as biology.

9.1 Kinship vs. Biology

Europeans and North Americans know that in their societies mating is not the same as marriage, although a valid marriage encourages mating between the partners. Similarly, all births do not constitute valid links of descent; in some societies, children whose parents have not been married according to accepted legal or religious specifications do not fit the cultural logic of descent, and many societies offer no positions that they can properly fill. Finally, not all acts of nurturance are recognized as adoption. Consider, for example, the status of foster parents in the United States, whose custody of the children they care for is officially temporary and can terminate if someone else clears the hurdles necessary to adopt those children legally.

Thus, mating, birth, and nurturance are ambiguous human experiences, and culturally constructed systems of kinship try to remove some of that ambiguity by paying selective attention to some aspects of these phenomena while downplaying or ignoring others. For example, one society may emphasize the female's role in childbearing and base its kinship system on this, paying little formal attention to the male's role in conception. Another society may trace connections through men, emphasizing the paternal role in conception and reducing the maternal role to that of passive incubator for the male seed. A third society may encourage its members to adopt not only children to rear but adult siblings for themselves, thus blurring the link between biological reproduction and family creation. Even though they contradict one another, all three understandings can be justified with reference to the panhuman experiences of mating, birth, and nurturance.

Every kinship system, therefore, emphasizes certain aspects of human reproductive experience and culturally constructs its own theory of human nature, defining how people develop from infants into mature social beings. Put another way, kinship is an *idiom:* a selective interpretation of the common human experiences of mating, birth, and nurturance. The result is a set of coherent principles that allow people to assign one another membership in particular groups. These principles normally cover several significant issues: how to carry out the reproduction of legitimate group members (marriage or adoption), where group members should live after marriage (residence rules), how to establish links between generations (descent or adoption), and how to pass on social positions (succession) or material goods (inheritance). Collectively, kinship principles define social groups, locate people within those groups, and position the people and groups in relation to one another both in space and over time. While this set of principles may be coherent, it is also open to modification, negotiation, and even legal challenge, as is shown by the ambiguities and questions raised by the consequences of **new reproductive technologies**—technologically mediated reproductive practices such as in vitro fertilization, surrogate parenthood, and sperm banks.

9.2 Descent

Discussions in anthropology tend to specialize in different aspects of kinship. Culturally defined connections based on mating are usually called *marriage* and are often referred to as *affinal* relationships (the term is based on *affinity,* which means "personal

[handwritten annotations: (consaguineal kin) → socially relivent / descent → "blood relations"]

attraction"). These relationships, which link a person to the kin of his or her spouse, will be discussed in the next chapter. In this chapter, we will consider culturally defined relationships based on birth and nurturance, which anthropologists traditionally call **descent.** People related to one another by descent are what English speakers often refer to as "blood" relations and are socially relevant connections based on either parent-child relationships or sibling relationships. Anthropologists use the term **consanguineal kin** to refer to all those people who are linked to one another by birth as blood relations (the word comes from the Latin *sanguineus,* meaning "of blood"). In addition, however, a consanguineal kinship group may include individuals whose membership in the group was established not by birth but by means of culturally specific rituals of incorporation that resemble what Euro-Americans call **adoption.** Incorporation via adoption often is seen to function in a way that parallels consanguinity, because it makes adopted persons and those who adopt them of the "same flesh." The transformation that incorporates adoptees frequently is explained in terms of *nurturance:* feeding, clothing, sheltering, and otherwise attending to the physical and emotional well-being of an individual for an extended period.

[handwritten margin note: adoption / welcoming/ accepting into group / crowd / becoming part of family unit]

Ethnographers have shown repeatedly that kinship bonds established by adoption can be just as strong as bonds established through birth. An interesting recent example comes from research among groups of gay and lesbian North Americans who established enduring "families by choice" that include individuals who are not sexual partners and who are unrelated by birth or marriage. Given that these chosen family ties are rooted in ongoing material and emotional support over extended periods of time, one might reasonably suggest that the people involved have based their relationships on nurturance and have "adopted" one another.

Because they are based on parent-child links that connect the generations, relations of descent have a time depth. In establishing patterns of descent, the cultures of the world rely on one of two basic strategies: either people are connected to one another through *both* their mothers and fathers, or they are connected by links traced *either* through the mother *or* the father, but not both.

9.3 Bilateral Descent

When people believe themselves to be just as related to their father's side of the family as to their mother's side, the term that is used is **bilateral descent** (this is sometimes also referred to as **cognatic descent**). Anthropologists have identified two different kinds of kinship groups based on bilateral descent. One is the *bilateral descent group*, an unusual form that consists of a set of people who claim to be related to one another through descent from a common ancestor, some through their mother's side and some through their father's; the other is the *bilateral kindred*, a much more common form that consists of all the relatives, related through males or females, of one person or group of siblings.

The **bilateral kindred** is the kinship group that most Europeans and North Americans know. A bilateral kindred forms around particular individuals and includes all the people linked to that individual through kin of both sexes—people usually called *relatives* in English. These people form a group only because of their connection to the central person, known in the terminology of kinship as *Ego*. In North American society, bilateral kindreds assemble at events associated with Ego: when he or she is baptized, confirmed, bar or bat mitzvahed, married, or buried. Each person within Ego's bilateral kindred has his or her own separate kindred. For example, Ego's father's sister's daughter has a kindred that includes people related to her through her father and her father's siblings—people to whom Ego is not related. This is simultaneously the major strength and major weakness of bilateral kindreds. That is, they have overlapping memberships, and they do not endure beyond the lifetime of an individual Ego. But they are widely extended, and they can form broad networks of people who are somehow related to one another.

Kinship systems create social relationships by defining sets of interlocking statuses and roles (defined in Chapter 6). Thus, a man

(handwritten: Rights + Obligations of kin - kinship = social interaction)

is to behave in the same way to all his "uncles" and in another way to his "father," and they are to behave to him as "nephew" and "son." (Perhaps he owes labor to anyone he calls "uncle" and is owed protection and support in return.) In anthropology, these are referred to as the *rights and obligations of kinship*. In a bilateral kindred, the "broad networks of people who are somehow related to one another" means that no matter where a person may be, if he or she finds kin there, the person and the kin have a basis for social interaction. This basis for interaction is different from the possible social interactions that the person might have with strangers (in this case, nonkin).

Organization in bilateral kindreds is advantageous when members of social groups need flexible ways of establishing ties to kin who do not live in one place. They are also useful when valued resources, such as farmland, are limited and every generation must be distributed across available plots in an efficient and flexible manner. Bilateral kindreds become problematic, however, in at least four kinds of social circumstances: when clear-cut membership in a particular social group must be determined, when social action requires the formation of groups that are larger than individual families, when conflicting claims to land and labor must be resolved, and when people are concerned with perpetuating a specific social order over time. In societies that face these dilemmas, unilineal descent groups usually are formed.

*(handwritten: * problems)*

(handwritten: Problems w/ bilateral kindreds —)

9.4 Unilineal Descent

The second major descent strategy, **unilineal descent**, is based on the principle that the most significant kin relationships must be traced through *either* the mother *or* the father but not both. Unilineal descent groups are found in more societies today than are any other kind. Those unilineal groups that are based on links traced through a person's father (or male kin) are called **patrilineal** (or **agnatic**); those traced through a mother (or female kin) are called **matrilineal** (or **uterine**). (Note that lineages are institutions —people do not choose whether they'd like to be patrilineal or matrilineal; these are the standardized long-established social

(handwritten: ① Father / ② Mother > lineages One or the other)

forms through which they learn about individuals and groups to whom they are related and how to interact with them.)

Unilineal descent groups are found all over the world. They are all based on the principle that certain kinds of parent-child relationships are more important than others. Membership in a unilineal descent group is based on the membership of the appropriate parent in the group. In a patrilineal system, an individual belongs to a group formed by links through males, the lineage of his or her father. In a matrilineal system, an individual belongs to a group formed by links through females, the lineage of his or her mother. "Patrilineal" and "matrilineal" do not mean that only men belong to one and only women to the other; rather, the terms refer to the principle by which membership is conferred. In a patrilineal society, women and men belong to a **patrilineage** formed by father-child links; similarly, in a matrilineal society, men and women belong to a **matrilineage** formed by mother-child connections. In other words, membership in the group is, in principle, unambiguous: an individual belongs to only one lineage. This is in contrast to a bilateral kindred, in which an individual belongs to overlapping groups.

Talk of patrilineal or matrilineal descent focuses attention on the kind of social group created by this pattern of descent: the lineage. A **lineage** is composed of all those people who believe they can specify the parent-child links that connect them to one another through a common ancestor. Typically, lineages vary in size from twenty or thirty members to several hundred or more.

Many anthropologists have argued that the most important feature of lineages is that they are corporate in organization. That is, a lineage has a single legal identity such that, to outsiders, all members of the lineage are equal in law to all others. In the case of a blood feud, for example, the death of any opposing lineage member avenges the death of the lineage member who began the feud; the death of the actual murderer is not required (feuding is defined in Chapter 7). Lineages are also corporate in that they control property, such as land or herds, as a unit.

Finally, lineages are the main political associations in the societies that have them. Individuals have no political or legal status in such societies except through lineage membership. They have relatives who are outside the lineage, but their own political and legal status derives from the lineage to which they belong.

Because membership in a lineage is determined through a direct line from father or mother to child, lineages can endure over time and in a sense have an independent existence. As long as people can remember their common ancestor, the group of people descended from that common ancestor can endure. Most lineage-based societies have a time depth that covers about five generations: grandparents, parents, Ego, children, and grandchildren.

When members of a descent group believe that they are in some way connected but cannot specify the precise genealogical links, they compose what anthropologists call a **clan**. Usually, a clan is made up of lineages that the larger society's members believe to be related to one another through links that go back to mythical times. Sometimes the common ancestor is said to be an animal that lived at the beginning of time. The important point to remember in distinguishing lineages and clans is that lineage members can specify the precise genealogical links back to their common ancestor ("Your mother was Eileen, her mother was Miriam, her sister was Rachel, her daughter was Ruth, and I am Ruth's son"), whereas clan members ordinarily cannot ("Our foremother was Turtle who came out of the sea when this land was settled. Turtle's children were many and for many generations raised sweet peas on our land. So it was that Violet, mother of Miriam and Rachel, was born of the line of the Turtle . . ."). The clan is thus larger than any lineage and also more diffuse in terms of both membership and the hold it has over individuals.

Lineages endure over time in societies in which no other form of organization lasts, and therefore, the system of lineages becomes the foundation of social life in the society. Although lineages might be the foundation of social life, however, this does not mean that they are immovable and inflexible. People can use lineage and clan membership to pursue their interests. Because lineage depth frequently extends to about five generations, the exact circumstances of lineage origins can be hazy and open to negotiation. Perhaps "Miriam" and "Rachel" from the preceding example have another sister whom everyone "forgot about" until someone appears who claims lineage membership as a descendant of the forgotten sister. If there are good reasons for including this descendant in the lineage, this claim might well be accepted.

By far the most common form of lineage organization is the patrilineage, which consists of all the people (male and female) who believe themselves to be related to one another because they are related to a common male ancestor by links through men. The prototypical kernel of a patrilineage is the father-son pair. Female members of patrilineages normally leave the lineage to marry, but women do not give up their membership in their own lineages. In a number of societies, women play an active role in the affairs of their own patrilineages for many years—usually until their interest in their own children directs their attention toward the children's lineage (which is, of course, the lineage of their father, the woman's husband).

By contrast, in a matrilineal society, descent is traced through women rather than through men. Superficially, a matrilineage is a mirror image of a patrilineage, but certain features make it distinct. First, the prototypical kernel of a matrilineage is the sister-brother pair—a matrilineage may be thought of as a group of brothers and sisters connected through links made by women. Brothers marry out and often live with the families of their wives, but they maintain an active interest in the affairs of their own lineage. Second, the most important man in a boy's life is not his father (who is not in his lineage) but his mother's brother, from whom he will receive his lineage inheritance. Third, the amount of power women exercise in matrilineages is still being hotly debated in anthropology. A matrilineage is not the same thing as a *matriarchy* (a society in which women rule); brothers often retain what appears to be a controlling interest in the lineage. Some anthropologists claim that the male members of a matrilineage are supposed to run the lineage, even though there is more autonomy for women in matrilineal societies than in patrilineal ones; they suggest that the day-to-day exercise of power tends to be carried out by the brothers or sometimes the husbands. A number of studies, however, have questioned the validity of these generalizations.

Trying to say something about matrilineal societies in general is difficult, since they vary a great deal. The ethnographic evidence suggests that matrilineages must be examined on a case-by-case basis.

9.5 Kinship Terminologies

Terminologies - aunt - refreance could be 4 diff people

People everywhere use special terms to address and refer to people they recognize as kin; anthropologists call these **kinship terminologies.** Consider the North American kinship term *aunt*. This term seems to refer to a woman who occupies a unique biological position, but in fact, it refers to a woman who may be related to a person in one of four different ways: as father's sister, mother's sister, father's brother's wife, or mother's brother's wife. From the perspective of North American kinship, all those women have something in common, and they are all placed into the same kinship category and called by the same kin term. Prototypically, one's aunts are women one generation older than oneself and are sisters or sisters-in-law of one's parents. However, North Americans may also refer to their mother's best friend as "aunt." By doing so, they recognize the strength of this system of classification by extending it to include fictive kin (also discussed in Chapter 6).

friends of family called aunt/ uncle etc.

Despite the variety of kinship systems in the world, anthropologists have identified six major patterns of kinship terminology based on how people categorize their cousins. The six patterns reflect common solutions to structural problems faced by societies organized in terms of kinship. They provide clues concerning how the vast and undifferentiated world of potential kin may be organized. Kinship terminologies suggest both the external boundaries and the internal divisions of the kinship groups, and they outline the structure of rights and obligations assigned to different members of the society.

The major criteria that are used for building kinship terminologies are listed here, from the most common to the least common:

◆ *Generation.* Kin terms distinguish relatives according to the **generation** to which the relatives belong. In English, the term *cousin* conventionally refers to someone of the same generation as Ego.

- *Gender.* The **gender** of the individual is used to differentiate kin. In Spanish, *primo* refers to a male cousin, and *prima* to a female cousin. In English, cousins are not distinguished on the basis of gender, but *uncle* and *aunt* are distinguished on the basis of both generation and gender.

- *Affinity.* A distinction is made on the basis of connection through marriage, or **affinity.** This criterion is used in Spanish when *suegra* (Ego's spouse's mother) is distinguished from *madre* (Ego's mother). In matrilineal societies, Ego's mother's sister and father's sister are distinguished from each other on the basis of affinity. The mother's sister is a direct, lineal relative, and the father's sister is an affine; they are called by different terms. *not direct*

- *Collaterality.* A distinction is made between kin who are believed to be in a direct line and those who are "off to one side," linked to Ego through a lineal relative. In English, the distinction of **collaterality** can be seen in the distinction between mother and aunt or between father and uncle.

- *Bifurcation.* **Bifurcation** distinguishes the mother's side of the family from the father's side. The Swedish kin terms *morbror* and *farbror* are bifurcating terms, one referring to the mother's brother and the other to the father's brother.

- *Relative age.* Relatives of the same category may be distinguished on the basis of **relative age**—that is, whether they are older or younger than Ego. Among the Ju/'hoansi of southern Africa, for example, speakers must separate "older brother" *(!ko)* from "younger brother" *(tsin).*

- *Sex of linking relative.* This criterion is related to collaterality. The **sex of linking relative** distinguishes cross relatives (usually cousins) from parallel relatives (also usually cousins). Parallel relatives are linked through two brothers or two sisters. **Parallel cousins,** for example, are Ego's father's brother's children or Ego's mother's sister's children. Cross relatives are linked through a brother-sister pair. **Cross cousins** are Ego's mother's brother's children or father's sister's children. The sex of either Ego or the cousins does not matter; the important factor is the sex of the linking relatives.

The six major patterns of kinship terminology that anthropologists have identified in the world are based on how cousins are classified. These patterns were named after the societies that represent the prototypes. The first two patterns discussed here are found in association with bilateral descent systems.

Bilateral Patterns   * Hawaiian Pattern - generation + gender

The **Hawaiian** pattern is based on the application of the first two criteria: generation and gender. The kin group is divided horizontally by generation, and within each generation are only two kinship terms, one for males and one for females (Figure 9.1). In this system, Ego maintains a maximum degree of flexibility in choosing the descent group with which to affiliate. Ego is also forced to look for a spouse in another kin group because Ego may not marry anyone in the same terminological category as a genetic parent, sibling, or offspring.

The **Eskimo** pattern reflects the symmetry of bilateral kindreds. A lineal core—the nuclear family—is distinguished from collateral relatives, who are not identified with the father's or the mother's side. Once past the immediate collateral line (aunts and uncles, great-aunts and great-uncles, nephews and nieces), generation is ignored. The remaining relatives are all "cousins," sometimes distinguished by *number* (second or third) or by *removal* (generations away from Ego[1]) (Figure 9.2). This is the only terminological system that sets the nuclear family apart from all other kin. If the Hawaiian system is like a cake made up of horizontal

Eskimo - nuclear family -> generation is ignored, all remaining relatives are cousins

---

[1] Ego's "first cousin once removed" can be one generation older or younger than Ego. For example, your cousin Suzanne's daughter is your first cousin once removed, but so is your father's cousin Arnold. Arnold's son, Eric, is your second cousin.

distinguished by #
or removal - generations
away from Ego.

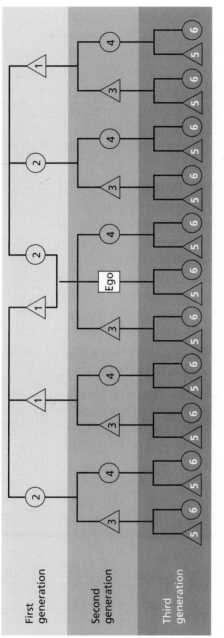

Figure 9.1 Hawaiian kinship terminology. Numbers represent kin terms. Ego uses the same kin term to refer to all those assigned the same number.

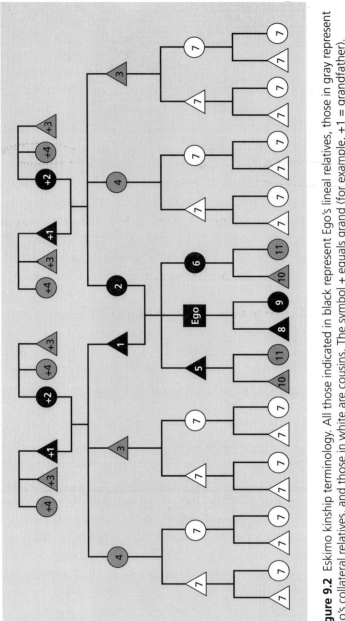

Figure 9.2 Eskimo kinship terminology. All those indicated in black represent Ego's lineal relatives, those in gray represent Ego's collateral relatives, and those in white are cousins. The symbol + equals grand (for example, +1 = grandfather).

layers of kin, this system is like an onion, with layers of kin surrounding a core.

Unilineal Patterns

[handwritten: Iroquois - bifurcate merging. Ego's mothers + fathers parallel siblings w/ Ego's parents]

The **Iroquois** pattern is sometimes known in the literature as **bifurcate merging,** because it merges Ego's mother's and father's parallel siblings with Ego's parents (Figure 9.3). The sex of the linking relatives is important in this system: The parents' parallel siblings are grouped together with the parents, whereas cross siblings are set apart. This is repeated on the level of cousins. In a bilateral system, these distinctions would be meaningless, but in a unilineal system, they mirror the lines of lineage membership. If Ego is a male, he will use one term to refer to all women of his matrilineage who are one generation older than he is. Their children are all referred to by another set of terms, one for males and one for females. Similarly, in his father's matrilineage, all men in the father's generation are referred to by one term. Their children are called by the same set of terms used for the cousins on the mother's side.

The **Crow** pattern is a matrilineal system named after the Crow people of North America, but it is found in many other matrilineal societies. This system distinguishes the two matrilineages that are important to Ego: Ego's own and that of Ego's father (Figure 9.4). As in the Iroquois system, the gender of the linking relative is important, and both parents and their same-sex siblings are grouped together. Their children—Ego's parallel cousins—are in the same category as Ego's siblings. The terms for cross cousins follow lineage membership, which is more important than generation. In Ego's own matrilineage, all the children of males are referred to by the same term regardless of their generation; their fathers are in Ego's matrilineage, but *they* are not. On the side of Ego's father's matrilineage, all male members are distinguished by one term, and all female members by another, regardless of generational relationship to Ego.

[handwritten margin: Crow — Ego's own + Ego's father]

[handwritten: Males + females distinguished by one term in relation to Ego.]

The system known as **Omaha,** found among some patrilineal peoples, is the mirror image of the Crow system. All the members of Ego's mother's patrilineage are distinguished only by gender,

[handwritten: Omaha - same as Crow system]

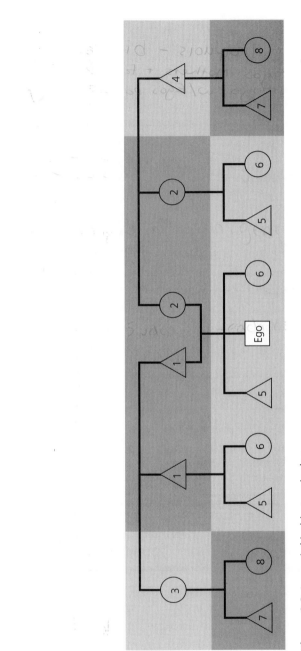

Figure 9.3 Iroquois kinship terminology.

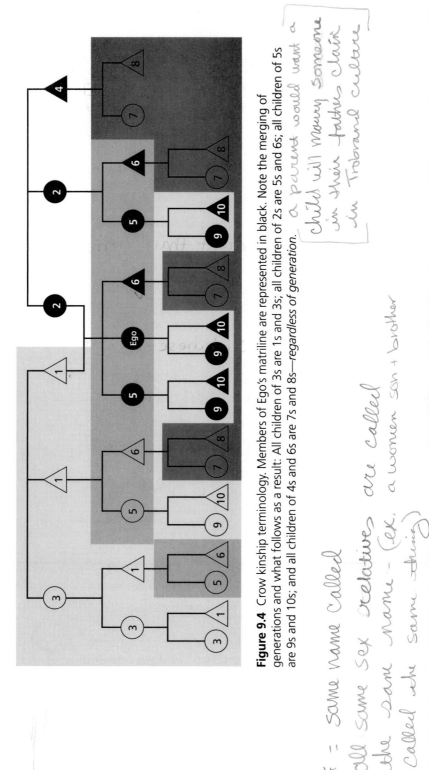

Figure 9.4 Crow kinship terminology. Members of Ego's matriline are represented in black. Note the merging of generations and what follows as a result: All children of 3s are 1s and 3s; all children of 2s are 5s and 6s; all children of 5s are 9s and 10s; and all children of 4s and 6s are 7s and 8s—*regardless of generation.*

= same name called

all same sex relatives are called
the same name – (ex. a woman son + brother
called the same thing)

a parent would want a
child will marry someone
in their father clair
in Trobrand culture

TABLE 9.1 Patterns of Kinship Terminology	
BILATERAL DESCENT	UNILINEAL DESCENT
Hawaiian	Iroquois
Eskimo	Crow
	Omaha
	Sudanese

Lineage more important than generation.

and all the children of women in Ego's patrilineage are referred to by the same term, one for males and one for females (Figure 9.5). Lineage membership again is more important than generation, a principle that often is hard for people living in bilateral kindreds to grasp.

Sudanese — each related person referred to by separate terms.

Finally, in the **Sudanese** pattern, each related person is referred to by a separate term (Figure 9.6). While this was originally seen as a relatively rare terminological pattern found in patrilineal societies, especially in northern Africa, it is also a very common pattern in South Asia and Southwest Asia, where it is found among speakers of Turkish, Arabic, Urdu, and Hindi, as well as other northern Indian languages. (Table 9.1 lists the basic patterns of kinship terminology.)

9.6 Summary

In this chapter, we looked at the enduring social connections that people build on the basis of mating, birth, and nurturance. We considered the different forms of descent—bilateral and unilineal—that are employed in different societies and looked at the logic of unilineal systems. Finally, we examined the principles that underlie the different sets of kinship terminologies that are found around the world and the six major forms of cousin terminologies revealed by comparative kinship studies.

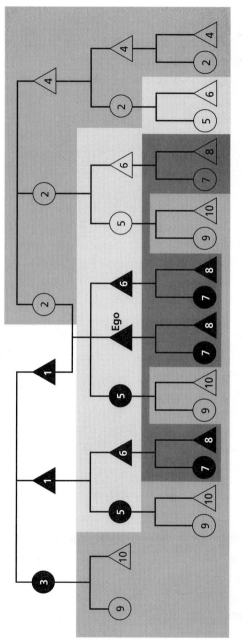

Figure 9.5 Omaha kinship terminology. Members of Ego's patriline are represented in black. Note the merging of generations and what follows as a result: All children of 4s are 2s and 4s; all children of 1s are 5s and 6s; all children of 6s are 7s and 8s; and all children of 3s and 5s are 9s and 10s—*regardless of generation.*

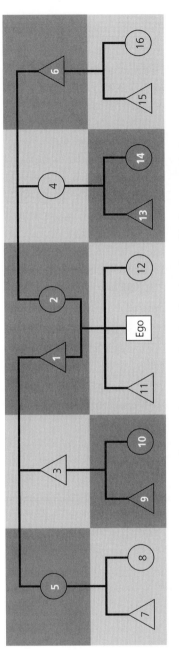

Figure 9.6 Sudanese kinship terminology. Each person related to Ego is referred to by a separate term.

For Further Reading

KINSHIP

Collier and Yanigasako 1987; Graburn 1971; Parkin 1997; Peletz 1995; Schneider 1968, 1984; Stone 1997, 2001

ADOPTION

Weismantel 1998

NEW REPRODUCTIVE TECHNOLOGIES

Strathern 1992

REPRODUCTION AND POWER

Ginsburg and Rapp 1995

10
Marriage and Family

The key terms and concepts covered in this chapter, in the order in which they appear:

marriage

exogamy

endogamy

neolocal

bilocal

patrilocal

virilocal

matrilocal

uxorilocal

avunculocal

ambilocal

monogamy

polygamy

plural marriage

polygyny

polyandry

bride service

bridewealth

dowry

hypergamy

sororate

levirate

family

conjugal family

nonconjugal family

nuclear family

polygynous family

extended families

joint families

blended family

family by choice

divorce

ANTHROPOLOGICAL DISCUSSIONS of marriage and the family complement discussions of descent and round out our study of kinship. As we saw in Chapter 9, the complexities and ambiguities of descent are many. The study of marriage and the family offers just as many complications, the first of which is how to define these terms.

10.1 What Is Marriage?

If we take what Euro-Americans call *marriage* as a prototype of a particular kind of social relationship, we discover in all societies institutions that resemble what people in the United States would call marriage. At the same time, the range of beliefs and practices associated with these institutions is broad, and the degree of overlap is not great. Nevertheless, we tend to classify all these institutions as *marriage* because of the key elements they do have in common. On these grounds, a prototypical **marriage** involves a man and a woman, transforms the status of the man and the woman, and stipulates the degree of sexual access the married partners may have to each other, ranging from exclusive to preferential. Marriage also establishes the legitimacy of children born to the wife and creates relationships between the kin of the wife and the kin of the husband.

We stress the prototypical nature of our definition because, although some societies are quite strict about allowing females to marry only males, and vice versa, other societies are not. The ethnographic literature contains many examples of marriage or marriagelike relationships that resemble the prototype in every respect except that the partners may be two men or two women (as defined according to biological sex criteria) or a living woman

depending on how its viewed - can be same sex marriages

and the ghost of a deceased male. Sometimes these marriages involve a sexual relationship between the partners; sometimes they do not. Apparently, the institution we are calling *marriage* has been viewed by members of many societies as so useful and valuable that they allow it to include partners of many different kinds—even though in all cases the prototype people have in mind seems to be a union between a man and a woman.

Examining the definition of marriage just offered, we note that marriage is a rite of passage: The parties go from the social status of single to the social status of married. In every society, this transformation of status is accompanied by adoption of new roles, but the rights and obligations associated with these roles vary enormously from culture to culture. Prototypically, among the rights and obligations of spouses are socially sanctioned sexual relations with each other. But, again, the nature and exclusivity of these sexual relations vary from culture to culture: some cultures insist that the partners may have sex only with each other; some view sexual encounters outside marriage less seriously for one partner (usually the husband) than for the other partner; and at least one culture allows the husband and wife to have sexual intercourse if they wish, but after spending one night together, they need never see each other again.

Cultural view-points on sexual relations)④

In most cultures, it is assumed that the married partners will have children, and the institution of marriage provides the children with a legitimate ascribed social status, based on who their parents are. In some cases, it is as if the father's and the mother's statuses were plotted on a graph, allowing the status of their child to be placed precisely in the social space where the *x*- and *y*-axes intersect; in other cases, the child's status depends solely on the position of one or the other parent. In addition, in most cultures, marriage creates formal relationships between the kin of the husband and the kin of the wife. By contrast, while mating may produce grandparents, it cannot produce in-laws or a formal relationship between the parents of the father and the parents of the mother. This aspect of marriage also has important social consequences.

⑤ marriage = legitimate ascribed social status

kin of husband + kin of wife formal relation- ships

10.2 Whom to Marry and Where to Live

Societies use kinship systems to exercise control over the marriages contracted by their members. When marriage rules specify that a person is to marry outside a defined social group—extended family, lineage, clan, class, ethnic group, or religious sect, for example—anthropologists say that the society in question practices **exogamy** (or *out-marriage*). The opposite situation—in which a person is expected to marry *within* a defined social group—is called **endogamy**. These patterns may be obligatory (i.e., strictly enforced) or merely preferred.

Once married, the spouses must live somewhere. Anthropologists have identified six patterns of postmarital residence. **Neolocal residence**, in which the new partners set up an independent household at a place of their own choosing, should be familiar to people who have grown up in the United States, Canada, and most of Europe. Neolocal residence tends to be found in societies that are more or less individualistic in their social organization, especially those in which bilateral kindreds also are found. Neolocal residence exists throughout the world but is most common in nation-states and in societies bordering the Mediterranean Sea. Some societies with bilateral kindreds have **bilocal** residence patterns, in which married partners live with (or near) either the wife's or the husband's parents. Despite this flexibility in allowing married partners to make decisions regarding where they might live, very few societies with bilocal residence have been described in the anthropological literature.

The most common residence pattern in the world, in terms of the number of societies in which it is practiced, is **patrilocal** residence, in which the partners in a marriage live with (or near) the husband's father. (In older anthropological writing, the term **virilocal** is sometimes used to distinguish residing with the husband's kin from residing specifically with the husband's father, for which the term *patrilocal* was reserved.) Patrilocal residence is strongly associated with patrilineal descent systems—about 85 percent of societies in which postmarital residence is patrilocal are also patrilineal. If children are born into a patrilineage and inherit from the father or other patrilineage members, then there are advantages to rearing them among the members of the lineage.

When the partners in a marriage live with (or near) the wife's mother, anthropologists use the term **matrilocal** residence. (Again, in older anthropological writing, the term **uxorilocal** is sometimes used to refer to residence with the wife's kin, as distinct from living with the wife's mother.) Matrilocal residence is found exclusively in matrilineal societies (some matrilineal societies are patrilocal). Anthropologists who study matrilineal societies have observed that sometimes the married partners live with the husband's mother's brother. This is based on the logic of matrilineal descent, in which the socially significant older male in a man's life is his mother's brother, because he is a member of the man's matrilineage while his own father is not. In these cases, anthropologists use the term **avunculocal** residence, building on the word *avuncular,* meaning "of uncles." As might be expected, avunculocal residence is found only in matrilineal societies, and, in contrast to matrilocal residence, it emphasizes the inheritance and labor patterns linking men in a matrilineage. A rare pattern called **ambilocal** residence is associated with ambilineal descent, in which the married partners may live with either the husband's or wife's group. This term is sometimes used interchangeably with the term *bilocal* and can be used to distinguish this pattern in unilineal societies from the pattern in bilateral societies.

10.3 How Many Spouses?

You may have noticed that we use the phrase married **partners** rather than the more common married **couple.** This is because the number of people who may be married to one another at the same time also varies across cultures. The major distinction is between societies that permit more than one spouse to a person and those that do not. A marriage pattern that permits a person to be married to only one spouse at a time is called **monogamy.** The term can also be used to refer to any marriage in which one person has only one spouse.

polyggamy - more than one spouse
plural marriage

The term **polygamy** is used to refer to marriage patterns in which a person may have more than one spouse, a practice also sometimes called **plural marriage.** Polygamy has two major forms: polygyny and polyandry. **Polygyny** is a marriage pattern in which a man may be married to more than one woman at a time. It is the most common of all marriage patterns in the world in terms of number of societies in which it is permitted. Polygyny enables a lineage, especially one with male children, to establish alliances with many other lineages through marriage. *creates stronger lineages*

polygyny
male can have more then one wife

In polygynous societies, it should be noted, not every man has more than one wife. In Islamic societies, for example, a man is permitted to have as many as four wives, but only on the condition that he can support them all equally well. Today, some Muslim authorities argue that "equal support" must be emotional as well as material. Furthermore, convinced that no man can feel exactly the same toward each of his wives, they have concluded that monogamy must be the rule. Other polygynous societies set no limit on the number of wives a man can marry. However, regardless of any limitations on the number of wives, polygynous societies are faced with a real **demographic** problem: because the number of men and women in any society is approximately equal, for every man with two wives, there is one man without a wife. To help solve this problem, men may be obliged to wait until they are older to marry, and women may be pressed to marry at a very young age; but even these practices do not completely eliminate the imbalance. As a result, polygyny is regularly connected with power in societies that practice it. That is, those men who are rich and powerful have multiple wives; those men who are poor and powerless either cannot marry, marry very late, have relationships outside of marriage, or marry women who are equally dispossessed.

demographic problems of unequal gender population

men who are rich = more wives

Polyandry, a pattern in which a woman is married to more than one man at a time, is the rarest of the three marriage patterns. In some polyandrous societies, a woman may marry several brothers. In others, she may marry men who are not related to one another and who all will live together in a single household. The tendency in polyandrous societies—especially in those in which a woman marries a set of brothers—is to intensify the connections

polyandry
women married to more than one man = RARE

↳ to intensify connections between lineages.

TABLE 10.1	Marriage Patterns	
MONOGAMY	POLYGAMY	
Monogamy	Polygyny	Polyandry

between lineages and to limit the number of potential heirs in the next generation, because no matter how many husbands a woman has, there is a limit to the number of offspring she can bear. (Table 10.1 lists basic marriage patterns.)

[handwritten: ★ Marriage = Alliance between 2 families / lineages]

10.4 Marriage as Alliance

In most societies, a marriage is an alliance between two families or lineages, not merely between two individuals, and it frequently requires traditional exchanges of wealth to legitimize it. These are usually characterized as bride service, bridewealth (or bride price), and dowry. In some societies, the prospective groom must work for the family of the bride for a predetermined length of time before they may marry, a practice called **bride service.** Other societies solemnize marriages with an exchange of **bridewealth:** certain symbolically important goods that are transferred from the immediate family of the groom (or his lineage) to the family of the bride (or her lineage) on the occasion of their marriage. *Symbolically important goods* include those things that are considered to be appropriate for exchange at a marriage in a specific society—for example, cattle, cash, shell ornaments, cotton cloth, or bird feathers. Bridewealth exchange is most common in patrilineal societies that combine agriculture, pastoralism, and patrilocal postmarital residence. Through their research in societies that exchange bridewealth, anthropologists have found that it is fundamentally incorrect to think of bridewealth as "buying" a wife. Rather, anthropologists view bridewealth as a way of compensating the bride's relatives for the loss of her labor and childbearing

[handwritten: exchange]

[handwritten: (M) bridewealth = compensation. to brides relatives bc/ they have lost her labor]

capacities. That is, when the bride goes to live with her husband and his lineage, she will be working and producing children for his people, not her own.

Bridewealth transactions create affinal relations between the relatives of the wife and those of the husband. The wife's relatives, in turn, use the bridewealth they receive for her to find a bride for her brother in yet another kinship group. In many societies in eastern and southern Africa, a woman gains power and influence over her brother because the cattle that her marriage brings allow him to marry and continue their lineage.

Dowry, by contrast, is typically a transfer of family wealth, usually from parents to their daughter, at the time of her marriage. It is found primarily in the agricultural societies of Europe and Asia, but it has been brought to some parts of Africa with the arrival of religions like Islam that support the practice. In societies in which both men and women are seen as heirs to family wealth, dowry is sometimes regarded as the way women receive their inheritance. Dowries often are considered the wife's contribution to the establishment of a new household, to which the husband may bring other forms of wealth or prestige. In stratified societies, the size of a woman's dowry frequently ensures that when she marries, she will continue to enjoy her accustomed style of life. In some stratified societies, an individual of lower status sometimes marries an individual of higher status, a situation in which the children will take on the higher status. This practice is called **hypergamy,** and it is usually one in which the lower status person is the wife and the dowry is seen (sometimes explicitly) as an exchange for the higher social position that the husband confers.

The ties that link kinship groups through marriage are sometimes so strong that they endure beyond the death of one of the partners. In some matrilineal and some patrilineal societies, if a wife dies young, the husband's line will ask the deceased wife's line for a substitute, often her sister. This practice, called the **sororate** (from the Latin *soror,* "sister"), is connected with both alliance strength and bridewealth. That is, both lines—that of the widower and that of the deceased wife—wish to maintain the alliance formed (and frequently continued) by the marriage. At

[handwritten: levirate - husband dies - wife re-marries her brother]

the same time, if a man marries the sister of his deceased wife, the bridewealth that his line gave to the line of the first wife will not have to be returned, so the disruption caused by the wife's death will be lessened. In many societies, if the husband dies the wife may (and in rare cases be obligated to) marry one of his brothers. This practice, called the **levirate** (from the Latin *levir,* "husband's brother"), is intended, like the sororate, to maintain the alliance between descent groups. In some societies, it also functions as a kind of social security system for widows, who might otherwise be destitute after the death of their husbands.

*[handwritten margin notes:
* family - women + children (dependent)
* conjugal - spousal pair + kids
* nonconjugal - women + kids]*

10.5 Family

Marriage frequently is understood, both by scholars and by the people who marry, as creating families. *Family* is another term that seeks to label a practice that is apparently universal but so variable as to make definition difficult. One minimal definition of a **family** would be that it consists of a woman and her dependent children. Some anthropologists prefer to distinguish the **conjugal family,** which is a family based on marriage—at its minimum, a husband and wife (a spousal pair) and their children—from the **nonconjugal family,** which consists of a woman and her children. In a nonconjugal family, the husband/father may be occasionally present or completely absent. Anthropologists note that nonconjugal families are never the only form of family organization in a society and, in fact, are usually rather infrequent. However, in some large-scale industrial societies, including the United States, nonconjugal families have become increasingly common. *[handwritten: due to divorce]* In most societies, the conjugal family is coresident—that is, spouses live in the same dwelling, along with their children—but in some matrilineal societies, the husband lives with his matrilineage, the wife and children live with theirs, and the husband visits his wife and children.

[handwritten margin: ex. Trobrianders]

Families can be characterized according to their structure. The neolocal, monogamous family is called the **nuclear family** and is composed of two generations, the parents and their unmarried children. In the nuclear family, each member has a series of evolving relationships with every other member: husband and wife,

[handwritten: nuclear family - 2 generations, parents + unmarried kids]

parents and children, and children with one another. These are the principal lines along which jealousy, controversy, and affection develop in neolocal monogamous families.

The **polygynous family** is composed of the husband, his cowives, and their children. The polygynous family adds complexity in the older generation not found in the nuclear family—the relationships among the cowives, and the relationship of the group of wives with the single husband. Additional complexity arises in the younger generation, as children have connections to half-siblings (the same father but a different mother) and full siblings (the same father and same mother), as well as an additional set of adults in their lives—their mother's cowives. These differences make the internal dynamics of polygynous families different from those of nuclear families.

The two family structures discussed so far are similar in that they are two generations in depth and involve one set of spouses (a man and a woman in the nuclear family, a man and his wives in a polygynous one). When families include a third generation—parents, married children, and grandchildren—anthropologists speak about **extended families**. When families maintain a two-generation depth but expand outward so that a set of siblings and their spouses and children lives together, anthropologists talk about **joint families.** Simply put, a joint family is composed of several brothers and their wives and children, or several sisters and their husbands and children. In societies in which they are found, extended and joint families are ideal patterns, which means that although people might want to live that way, not everyone is able to.

In recent years in the United States, anthropologists have observed the emergence of new family types. The **blended family** occurs when previously divorced people marry, bringing with them children from their previous marriages. The internal dynamics of the new family—which can come to include his children, her children, and their children—may sometimes have some similarities to the dynamics of polygynous families. Specifically, the relations among the children and their relations to each parent may be

TABLE 10.2   Types of Families

NONCONJUGAL FAMILIES	CONJUGAL FAMILIES	FAMILIES BY CHOICE
Mother and children	Nuclear	Enduring ties that are
	Polygynous	not the product of
	Extended	heterosexual marriage
	Joint	
	Blended	

complex and negotiated over time. (Table 10.2 summarizes the basic family types.)

A second new form is the **family by choice,** *gay marriages* a term used by some GLBT (Gay, Lesbian, Bisexual, Transgender) people to refer to families that are not the product of heterosexual marriage. Derived from a model that resembles kinship based on nurturance (defined in Chapter 9), some North American GLBT people argue that "whatever endures is real." As a result, the group of people that endures—which may include some or all of the kin of each member of the couple, their close friends, and children of either member or children who may be adopted—forms a family. GLBT activists have used this model as a resource in their struggle to obtain for long-standing families of choice some of the same legal rights enjoyed by traditional heterosexual families, such as hospital visiting privileges, partner insurance coverage, joint adoption, and property rights.

Marriages do not always last forever, and almost all societies make it possible for married couples to divorce—that is, to dissolve the marriage in a socially recognized way, regulating the status of those who were involved with the marriage and any offspring of the marriage. In some societies, it is not merely the people who were married who are involved in the divorce; it may also include other family or lineage members of the divorcing parties whose relationships are also changed by the divorce. In societies in which bridewealth is part of the marriage ceremony, for example, divorce may cause difficulties if the bridewealth must be returned. In such societies, a man who divorces a wife or whose wife leaves him expects her family to return to him some of the bridewealth he offered in exchange for her. But the wife's family may well have exchanged the bridewealth they received when she married to obtain wives for her brothers. As a result, her brothers' marriages may have to be broken up in order to recoup enough bridewealth from their in-laws to repay their sister's ex-husband or his line. Sometimes a new husband will repay the bridewealth to the former husband's line, thus letting the bride's relatives off the hook.

Grounds for divorce vary from society to society, as does which party may initiate divorce. Common grounds for divorce often include nagging, quarreling, cruelty, violence, stinginess, and adultery. Cross-culturally, a frequent ground for divorce is childlessness.

Families break apart and new households form in other ways besides divorce. In joint families, for example, the pressures that build up among coresident brothers or sisters often increase dramatically on the death of the father. In theory, the eldest son inherits the position of head of household from his father, but his younger brothers may not accept his authority as readily as they did the father's. Some younger brothers may decide to establish their own households, and so the joint family gradually splits. Each brother whose household splits off from the joint stem usually hopes to start his own joint family; eventually, his sons will bring their wives into the household, and a new joint family emerges out of the ashes of an old one.

10.6 Summary

In this chapter, we looked at a five-part prototype of marriage that enables anthropologists to identify this social form cross-culturally. We also considered the great variety of beliefs and practices associated with what English speakers call marriage. We touched on postmarital residence rules and rules concerning the number of spouses a person may have. We looked at the economic aspects of marriage and the ways in which the social obligations it creates may be maintained beyond the death of one of the partners. Finally, we examined the family and the patterns of family structure that people use to establish and sever social relationships when necessary.

For Further Reading

Many of the readings for Chapter 9 also deal with marriage and family. Here are some readings specific to these topics:

MARRIAGE

Goody and Tambiah 1973; Levine 1988; Sacks 1979; Schuler 1987

FAMILY

Netting, Wilk, and Arnould 1984; Weston 1991

11

Globalization and the Culture of Capitalism

The key terms and concepts covered in this chapter, in the order in which they appear:

colonialism	modernization theory	diaspora
neocolonialism	revolutionary movements	globalization
corvee	alienation proletarianization	cyberculture
cultural imperialism		postmodern condition
westernization	dependency theory	identity politics
internal colonialism	international political economy	cultural pluralism accommodated
acculturation		
syncretism	world system theory	human rights
cargo cults	core	cultural rights
assimilate	periphery	ethnocide
subaltern	semiperiphery	genocide
nationalism	deterritorialization	

ANTHROPOLOGISTS HAVE SPECIALIZED in taking seriously the ways of life of people in "remote" parts of the world—remote, that is, from the activities and concerns of most people in the Western capitalist nations from which the anthropologists traditionally came. Until very recently, limitations rooted in the technologies of transportation and communication meant that, even when political or economic ties linked territories at some distance from one another, the movement of people or goods or ideas from one place to another was slow and cumbersome. By 5000 years ago, the growth of states and their expansion into empires drew peoples in several regions of the world into intensified contact with one another. At the end of the twentieth century, however, economic or political events whose consequences used to be felt only within restricted geographical regions regularly affected people living in regions of the world that used to be considered remote from one another. It was only a little over five centuries ago that European explorers began to make contact, and then to conquer, indigenous groups on all continents, eventually establishing far-flung colonial empires that lasted until the middle of the twentieth century. The relationships established by European colonial domination created the conditions for the emergence, by the end of the twentieth century, of a fully integrated global economy.

11.1 Colonialism and the Study of Culture Change

Europeans did not invent **colonialism,** which can be defined as political conquest of one society by another, followed by social domination and forced cultural change. Since the rise of the first states in antiquity, regions of varying sizes have been brought together in different parts of the world as a result of imperial expansion, and what is today western Europe was marginal to most of them. None of those earlier empires, however, ever attained the scope of the European colonial empires, especially during their period of greatest expansion, which stretched roughly from the end of the nineteenth century until shortly after World War II, when European colonies began to gain their independence. At that time, many observers hoped that the relationships of subjugation between colonizer and colonized would dissolve. They hoped that different geographical regions of former empires would regain the kind of autonomy that had so often followed the breakup of empires in the past. Such hopes were dashed, however, when the ties between former colonies and their former imperial rulers not only did not disappear after independence but instead often reappeared in the form of "consultancies" to the new governments. These persisting relationships in the absence of imperial political domination have often been called neocolonialism, and social scientists have struggled to explain why they are so resilient.

Many scholars, anthropologists included, decided that neocolonial ties were basically economic in nature and that their strength came from an international division of labor that colonialism itself had established. Once certain geographical regions within an empire became specialized in specific economic tasks within the imperial economy, the argument went, those relationships became very difficult, if not impossible, to dislodge, even when the empire itself no longer existed. Much evidence was collected to document the forced social and cultural change wrought on the economic, social, and cultural lives of colonized peoples in order to create this international division of labor during the period of European colonial rule.

The European empires of the past two centuries were, by and large, not made up of settler colonies. Except for select areas like southern or eastern Africa for the British or Morocco and Algeria for the French, European soldiers and administrators were always relatively limited in number; the colonizers relied on superior military technology, rather than sheer numbers, to impose their will. They were neither able nor, in most cases, interested in remaking colonized societies from top to bottom, but they did institute certain changes that would make it easier for them to achieve the economic goals that were their primary motivation. Thus, large tracts of land were regularly appropriated from colonized peoples for the purpose of resource extraction (mining, for example) or for growing cash crops valued in Europe (see Chapter 8 for further discussion of cash crops), displacing indigenous farmers and herders from their lands and turning them into wage-workers forced to seek employment on plantations, in mines, or in the growing cities. Economic efficiency further required the building of infrastructure (roads, ports, etc.) by which cash crops or minerals could be transported out of colonies and back to Europe. Colonists regularly relied on the labor of colonized peoples to build such infrastructure, sometimes resorting to the use of **corvee,** or <u>forced labor,</u> in which laborers were required to work a given number of days on a given project or risk fines or imprisonment.

As colonial economic control increased, colonized peoples became familiar with European economic practices such as the use of money to purchase commodities or the production of goods for exchange. Adopting wage work and purchasing goods to meet subsistence needs increasingly became a necessity, as people were deprived of the land on which they formerly had grown subsistence crops or as their traditional artisanal production of pots or cloth or farm implements was supplanted by manufactured items produced in and imported from Europe. Over time, indigenous peoples had to come to terms with these cultural practices, and the way they did so has varied from time to time and place to place. They were coping with what many scholars have called **cultural imperialism,** a situation in which the ideas and practices of one culture are imposed upon other cultures, which may be modified or eliminated as a result. Western colonialism appeared to produce a distinctive kind of cultural imperialism, frequently called **westernization,** in which the ideas and practices of western European (or North American) culture eventually displaced many of the ideas and practices of the indigenous cultures of the colonies. In places where European settler colonies eventually broke from Europe, as in North, Central, and South America, anthropologists often speak of **internal colonialism** imposed on indigenous peoples within the borders of independent states.

11.2 The Cultural Effects of Contact

Anthropologists probably have always been aware that the non-Western societies in which they were doing fieldwork had been heavily affected by imperialist forces of one kind or another. This awareness was surely responsible at least in part for the relativistic defense of bounded, internally harmonious "cultures" so important in the early twentieth century. Anthropologists like Margaret Mead and Bronislaw Malinowski, for example, regularly drew attention to what they saw as the misguided and pernicious effects of colonizers and missionaries on indigenous cultures. Shortly before his death, Malinowski wrote about the enormous changes taking place in indigenous cultures as a result of colonialism, and American anthropologists like Melville Herskovits were drawing attention to the processes of cultural change that colonial encounters (external and internal) had set in motion. It was only after World War II, however, and especially after the achievement of political independence by former European colonies, that the colonial situation itself became an explicit focus of ethnographic study.

When anthropologists began to address the consequences of cultural contact, they invented a new vocabulary to try to describe the processes that seemed to be at work. In the United States, Herskovits and his colleagues spoke of **acculturation:** a process by which cultures in contact borrow ideas and practices from one another, thereby modifying or replacing traditional ideas and practices. The study of cultural borrowing had always been important in North American anthropology, and anthropologists pointed out that the process often involved reshaping the borrowed item in order to make it fit into preexisting cultural arrangements. When viewed by an outside observer, the result often was described as **syncretism:** a mixing of elements from two or more traditions. For example, when missionary Christianity and a traditional indigenous religious system both contribute to new shared spiritual practices that are neither wholly "Christian" nor wholly "traditional" (see Chapter 5), that is syncretism.

Frequently cited examples of religious syncretism are the so-called cargo cults that developed in Melanesia and New Guinea in the decades after colonial conquest, many of them stimulated by contact with the United States military during World War II. The "cargo" refers, in general, to the abundant manufactured goods brought to the islands by Western missionaries, traders, and soldiers. Although cargo cults differed in many specifics of belief and practice, they had in common the mixture of Christian religious doctrine and traditional indigenous beliefs about their ancestors. A key feature was the belief that the ancestors would return on ships or planes, bringing for their kin the cargo that Europeans possessed in such abundance. In some places, members of the cargo cult even constructed models of airplanes or control towers that had the ritual function of enticing the ancestors and their cargo.

Acculturation theorists realized that processes of cultural borrowing and modification might be mutual—with the partners involved taking from and giving to one another on an equal, unconstrained basis—or that they could be skewed in one direction only, as a result of unequal power relations. The latter situation could often be found under colonial rule. For example, children in colonies frequently were taken from their home villages and taught the colonizer's language and culture in boarding schools deliberately designed to cut children off from the influence of their families' traditional way of life. In such cases, the goal was often explicitly to "civilize" the children, which in the circumstances meant to replace the children's culture with that of the colonizer. That is, the colonizers wanted these children to **assimilate** to colonial society and culture, to cut off identification with their culture of origin and become totally absorbed in the ways of Europeans. Pressure to assimilate is not unique to colonial situations; it is commonly encountered by refugee or immigrant groups moving into societies dominated by cultural traditions very different from their own. In both cases, however, the goal of assimilation is the

↓ Goal of assimilation

same: the disappearance of distinctive cultural features that set the lower-ranking and less influential **subaltern** groups apart from those privileged and powerful groups who dominate them.

11.3 Analyzing Sociocultural Change in the Postcolonial World

Assimilation - Ⓜ * Setting lower/upper powerful groups apart

The contradiction inherent in most colonial policies urging cultural assimilation, however, was that even the most highly "assimilated" members of colonized societies could never hope to be treated as equals by their colonial masters. This realization by growing numbers of educated members of subaltern groups helped fuel the movement for independence from colonial control, which gained momentum after World War II. By virtue of their shared colonial history and their shared rejection of domination, independence leaders argued that they and their followers had developed a distinct sense of themselves as "a people" or "nation," an orientation that came to be called **nationalism.** Nationalist leaders in colonies claimed that colonized peoples, like other "nations" of the world, had a right to political self-determination; that is, they were entitled to become independent nation-states.

* remaining distinct

nationalism

In the postcolonial world of the 1950s and early 1960s, the leaders of many newly independent nation-states were hopeful that their countries could escape the impoverished status they had occupied under colonial rule. Although such leaders rejected the notion that their citizens needed to become "civilized," they were committed to the idea that their societies needed "development" and "modernization." Many economists in Western nations agreed with them. In a manner reminiscent of Lewis Henry Morgan, these economists subscribed to a unilineal theory of economic development, often referred to as **modernization theory.** They studied the economic histories of the first nations in the world to "develop" or to "modernize"—that is, to create economies based on industrial production and capitalist business practices. Some economists believed that they had discovered a universal recipe for modernization that would guarantee economic development in any new nation that followed their advice.

Ⓒ leaders of nationalistic states knew they had to become modernized + develop

* Modernization Theory -> Capitalists / industrial production economies

Modernization theory did not view industrial capitalism as a distinctive cultural system but rather as the most highly developed economic system yet produced on the face of the earth. It assumed that "nations" were units that passed naturally through stages of economic growth at different rates and that the more "mature" nations ought to assist the "young" nations to attain maturity. However, economists from Western industrial nations insisted that the leaders of new nations carefully follow their recipe for development. Like parents dealing with sometimes unruly adolescent children, they worried that young nations eager to modernize might resist disciplined evolution through the stages of economic growth and look for a shortcut to economic prosperity.

During the Cold War years, when modernization theory developed, the tempting shortcut was seen as socialist revolution. The twentieth century has been marked by a series of revolutions all over the globe, the best known being those in Mexico, Russia, China, Vietnam, Algeria, Cuba, and Nicaragua. In 1969, anthropologist Eric Wolf characterized all but the last revolution on this list (which would take place ten years later) as wars waged by peasants to defend themselves from the disruptions caused in their societies by capitalist market penetration. Following the Russian Revolution, opponents of the capitalist system elsewhere in the world also formed **revolutionary movements** whose explicit aim was to throw capitalists out of the country by force. Although many rank-and-file members of the revolutionary movements had modest dreams of return to a more prosperous status quo ante, their leaders often hoped to replace capitalism with some locally appropriate form of socialist society. After the successful Cuban Revolution in 1959, when Fidel Castro and his supporters openly committed themselves to socialism and allied with the Soviet Union, modernization theory became the foreign-policy option of choice in the United States, a potentially powerful approach to economic development that might woo potential revolutionaries elsewhere away from the Marxist threat (see Chapter 8).

The Marxist threat was real because Marxists argued that the factor responsible for the impoverished economies of postcolonial states was precisely what the modernization theorists were offer-

[handwritten: Capitalism = Seperation/Alienation of workers from tools, raw materials etc.]

ing as a cure, namely, capitalism (see Chapter 8 for a detailed discussion). A key feature of capitalism is the way it creates separation, or **alienation,** of workers from the tools, raw materials, and technical knowledge required to produce goods. When, for example, peasants are pushed off the land and forced to work for wages in mines or on commercial farms, they are caught up in a process sometimes called **proletarianization:** a process of class formation that transforms people deprived of subsistence resources into workers at the bottom of the capitalist political economy.

[handwritten: Creates Class Seperation]

Once these transformed relations of production are well entrenched, political independence alone will not make them go away. For example, successful commercial plantations will not automatically be dismantled so that peasants can reclaim lands to farm, because the landlords (whether outsiders or locals) will be unwilling to give up the wealth that can be accumulated by using wage laborers to produce cash crops for the international capitalist market. This, it is argued, is why political independence brought neocolonialism rather than economic independence to so many parts of the world. The economies and cultures of colonized peoples had been so thoroughly remade under capitalist colonialism that cutting off all ties to former masters would have resulted in economic catastrophe.

In the 1960s, Latin American economists and sociologists were trying to understand why their nations, free of official colonial domination for over a century, were no better off than the newly independent states of Africa. Articulating an analytic framework that came to be called **dependency theory,** they argued that poverty and "underdevelopment" were a *consequence* of capitalist colonial intervention in otherwise thriving independent societies, and not some original lowly state in which colonized territories had been languishing until the colonizers arrived. Capitalist colonialism *reduced* colonies to a state of underdevelopment in which their economies came to depend on decisions made outside their borders by colonial rulers who were promoting their own interests, not the interests of the colonies. Indeed, they argued, the "development" of rich countries depended on the deliberate impoverishment of other parts of the world.

[handwritten: Dependency → Theory | (s) rich countries depend on the impoverished parts of the world to become/stay wealthy.]

From this perspective, capitalist recipes for economic "development" could hardly be the solution to "underdevelopment," for capitalism had created the underdevelopment in the first place. Dependency theory offered a new angle from which to consider such phenomena as cargo cults. Rather than being viewed simply as fascinating, syncretic products of culture contact, cargo cults began to look like creative attempts by colonized groups deprived of the promised benefits of capitalist colonialism to make sense of their deprivation and to overcome it by innovative religious means.

Modernization theory and dependency theory differ on many points. Modernization theory not only views capitalist entrepreneurship as the key to self-sustaining economic growth but also personifies nation-states as primordial sociocultural units, each of which is individually responsible for its own successful modernization. Thus, the individualism at the center of capitalist culture reappears in modernization theory, in which individual nation-states must pursue their own economic self-interest in competition with one another. Dependency theory, by contrast, rejects the individualistic analysis along with its conclusions. Nation-states are *not* primordial entities but are historical creations; and some nations of the world were able to become powerful and rich only because they forced other societies into weakness and poverty. The fates of a rich country and its poor colonies (or neocolonies) are thus intimately interrelated. Social-scientific perspectives that take this observation as their starting point usually are said to pay attention to an **international political economy** (see Chapter 7).

An ongoing struggle between anthropologists favorable to modernization theory and those critical of it was a feature of the Cold War years of the 1950s and 1960s. By the 1970s, critics of modernization theory were active in anthropology, many of them influenced by dependency theory. By the 1980s, however, many anthropologists agreed that dependency theory was too simplistic to account for the complexities of the postcolonial world. Many anthropologists thus adopted the broader perspective of **world system theory,** an analytical framework first suggested in the 1970s by sociologist Immanuel Wallerstein.

World system theory expanded upon and strengthened the Marxist critique of capitalist colonialism inherent in dependency theory. Wallerstein's most original idea was to apply a functionalist analytic framework (see Chapter 12) to the capitalist world system, which was, in his opinion, the only social system that came close to being self-contained and self-regulating in the structural-functionalist manner. Wallerstein stressed that capitalism was a *world* system, not because it included the entire world but because the system incorporated territories scattered across the globe in order to maintain itself and to grow. Unlike empires, which in the past had united far-flung territories under a single political authority, the capitalist world system united far-flung territories *by economic means alone* through the capitalist market.

Modernization theorists, as we noted, conceive of nation-states as autonomous actors ranked in various positions along a continuum from "backward"/"underdeveloped"/"less developed" and so on to "developed" industrial economies. By contrast, analysts who adopted a world system perspective use a different terminology, classifying nation-states and other political entities in terms of the role they play within the world system's international division of labor. Thus, those countries that are fully industrialized, monopolize technological expertise and innovation, control financial decision-making for the system as a whole, and pay relatively high wages to skilled workers are said to belong to the **core** of the world system. Core nations today include the former European colonial powers, the United States, and Japan. By contrast, those countries whose main contributions to capitalism are raw materials for industries in the core and expanding markets for manufactured goods are said to belong to the **periphery** of the world system. The ranks of peripheral nations are dominated by former colonies. Finally, some countries are said to belong in the **semiperiphery**; these nations either were once part of the core or look as though they might someday be able to move into the core. In recent years, China, India, Brazil, and Indonesia often have been considered semiperipheral by world system theorists.

World system theory has established itself within anthropology as a powerful analytic framework for making sense of recent historical developments in the global political economy and their effects on the local communities in which anthropologists have traditionally carried out fieldwork. Thinking in terms of world systems, rather than empires, has also changed the way historians and social scientists approach world history outside Europe prior to the rise of capitalism. Geographer Janet Abu-Lughod, for example, has made a persuasive case for the existence of a thirteenth-century world system centered in India that organized trade by land and sea from Southeast Asia to Western Europe and from China to East Africa. Some anthropologists have been inspired by Abu-Lughod's work, not only because it provides a fuller historical context for understanding the development of cultures they study in the lands that formerly belonged to this world system, but also because it shows that the capitalist world system is not the only world system ever to exist and that Western cultural hegemony is not inevitable.

11.4 Post–Cold War Changes

Following the end of the Cold War in 1989, however, cultural anthropologists were among the social scientists who observed a series of far-reaching and intensifying global changes. From one point of view, it looked as though the fall of socialism in the former Soviet Union and the adoption of capitalist economic practices in China was making it possible for the capitalist world system literally to swallow up the entire world. From another point of view, however, the forces that were responsible for these new interconnections appeared to be so powerful that they were undermining key features of the world system.

For example, world system theory rests on the assumption of an international division of labor in which people in different geographical regions specialize in different economic tasks. This makes it both possible and meaningful to distinguish core from semiperipheral from peripheral nations. However, the vast improvements in transportation and communication technologies in recent decades has permitted a breakdown in the link between economic role and territory. Anthropologists have described a massive **deterritorialization** of both peoples and activities from their former exclusive locations in one or another region of the world system. Anthropologists face the challenge of carrying out fieldwork among people whose ancestors may have been rooted in a single territory but who themselves may be living in a **diaspora,** located in many different, and distant, places in the world. Whereas in the past, such movements of peoples encountered many barriers, demand for certain kinds of workers in core countries has promoted migration, both legal and illegal, of people from periphery to core.

At the same time, technology-dependent manufacturing activities that used to take place exclusively in the core have been relocated in peripheral nations to take advantage of low wage rates. Wage work in manufacturing formerly enabled citizens of core nations with little formal education to earn middle-class incomes; the cost and inconvenience of moving factories out of the core meant that workers could bargain for higher wages and greater benefits with some success. Today's cutting-edge manufacturing plants, however, can be shipped to peripheral countries and quickly set up. They can also be quickly dismantled, in order to move them elsewhere in the periphery where labor costs are lower. Although the manufacturing jobs that have been deterritorialized out of the core are welcome in poor peripheral countries, the loss of such jobs in core countries has caused severe hardship and dislocation for the newly unemployed.

11.5 Globalization

The intensifying flow of capital, goods, people (tourists as well as immigrants and refugees), images, and ideas around the world has come to be called **globalization.** People need not ever leave their homes, however, to be buffeted by the forces of globalization. The explosive development of computer technology, e-mail communication, and the Internet has linked people who have never seen one another into global networks, or *virtual communities,* that reach beyond the boundaries of nation-states. Many anthropologists have become interested in the growth of **cyberculture:** the

Cyber - Culture ✓

distinct beliefs and practices developing in connection with the
growth of computer-mediated communication. The cultural possibilities that might be produced by unbridled cyberexchanges on a
global level remain limited, however, because access to computer-
mediated communication is still largely the preserve of middle-
class users with mastery of computer technology and literacy in
English. In addition, various national governments continue to try
to restrict their citizens' access to cybercommunication, with varying degrees of success.

Anthropologists have also begun to look at popular culture
and mass media as important sites where global processes and
local interpretations meet in interesting and significant ways.
Studies of television serials in Egypt and India have examined
viewers' reactions to the programs, especially with regard to gender, regional identity, and class. Five different anthropologists
have each studied McDonald's in one of five different countries in
Asia to find the ways in which the company, its restaurants, and
its products and practices (birthday parties, for example)—seen by
many people around the world as a symbol of cultural imperialism of the United States—are incorporated into people's everyday
experiences.

As the preceding discussion illustrates, the forces of globalization have little respect for the kinds of social, cultural, religious,
political, and geographical boundaries that are used to discipline
and routinize contacts between vastly different categories of
ideas, images, practices, and peoples. Thus, globalization and its
consequences are an excellent illustration of what many anthropologists and other scholars describe as the **postmodern condition.** This term refers to the situation in which human beings find
themselves at the dawn of the twenty-first century, when all the
old certainties, categories, and standards associated with *rational
scientific modernity* seem to be breaking down, in large part
because the supposed benefits of commitment to modernity—
prosperity, equality, peace—seem more elusive today than ever
(see Chapter 1).

Since 1989, for example, the certainties of the Cold War years
have given way to bewilderment for many citizens of the United

States: Who are our enemies now? Who are our friends? Indeed, who are "we" and who are "they"? Culture change, migration, and tourism bring together what used to be separate and pull apart what used to appear uniform. Such a situation of uncertainty and insecurity has given rise to a phenomenon sometimes called identity politics: struggles by groups to create and sustain exclusionary political alliances defined more narrowly than, and often in opposition to, a common identity as citizens of a nation-state. Although neither the nation-state nor citizenship has disappeared, many groups and individuals clearly refuse to accept them as overriding standards beneath which all other communities and identities should be subordinated or eliminated. Put another way, the hegemony of the nation-state and citizenship has been challenged.

The postmodern challenge of identity politics exposes the fact that societies and cultures that have been portrayed, either by their members or by outsiders, as homogenous and harmonious are more often characterized by cultural pluralism. That is, they are made up of a multiplicity of heterogenous subgroups whose ways of thinking and living vary, whose interests may be opposed, and whose cooperation is not automatic. Although coercion by ruling elites may give the appearance of cultural uniformity, pluralism emerges when coercion weakens. It becomes apparent that some members of a society have serious reservations about the values and practices they have been pressured to accept. That is, rather than having willingly adopted, or assimilated to, the dominant majority culture, they have merely **accommodated** themselves to it.

In a globalized world, in which people in many peripheral countries have become familiar with the ideology of individual **human rights** developed in powerful core cultures, local groups may claim that they have been deprived of their natural rights to life, liberty, or property. They often find allies in core nations who support their demands that their human rights as individuals be respected. Such claims frequently have been made by citizens of nations whose leaders signed the United Nations Declaration on Human Rights but who find their own rights being violated by those same leaders.

[handwritten: Respect for all rights minorities etc.]

When minority groups are subject to coercive attempts at cultural assimilation, they may resist and demand that the wider society respect not only their individual human rights but also the shared **cultural rights** of the group to which they belong. The argument has been made in recent years, in national and international legal forums, that cultural groups have rights of their own, distinct from the rights of their individual members. Such cultural rights usually include whatever is seen as necessary to keep the group's culture viable, such as adequate economic and political resources to preserve their values and practices, including their language, and pass them on to future generations. Indeed, international debates over human rights—individual versus group rights, political and civil rights versus socioeconomic rights, rights as defined by nation-states versus the right of self-determination by indigenous and other minority groups within their borders—show that defining human rights is an ongoing multicultural project of global proportions.

[handwritten left margin: Conflict over human rights issues →]

That claims for cultural rights, as well as individual rights, are taken seriously at the beginning of the twenty-first century often is seen as evidence for the postmodern circumstances in which we live. Sociopolitical entities like nation-states, however, depend for their legitimacy on their being run by representatives of the "nation." The pressures to assimilate recalcitrant minorities may range from **ethnocide,** or the deliberate destruction of a cultural tradition, to **genocide,** or the mass murder of an entire social or cultural group whose presence is seen as threatening to those who run a state, as has been documented in Nazi Germany, Rwanda, the former Yugoslavia, and elsewhere.

*[handwritten: * ethnocide = destruction of a cultural tradition]*
*[handwritten: * genocide = mass murder of social/cultural group]*

11.6 Summary

In this chapter, we concentrated on the effect that one part of the world—the capitalist world—has had on other parts of the world. At the same time, we considered the ways in which different societies have responded to external pressures, ranging from assimilation to revolutionary movements. We discussed several of the approaches taken by anthropologists and other scholars in thinking about the encounters of different peoples with different political economic systems, which led to a consideration of globalization and the postmodern condition. Finally, we touched on ethnocide and genocide, still all too common in the world, and on human and cultural rights.

For Further Reading

OVERVIEW
Kearney 1995; Robbins 1999

COLONIALISM
Pels 1997

REFUGEES, GENOCIDE, AND HUMAN RIGHTS
Daniel and Knudsen 1995; Malkki 1995; Messer 1993; Nagengast 1994

GLOBALIZATION
Abu-Lughod 1989; Appadurai 1996; Featherstone 1990; Hannerz 1996

DEPENDENCY AND DEVELOPMENT
Lewellen 1995

12

Theory in Cultural Anthropology

The key terms and concepts covered in this chapter, in the order in which they appear:

material phenomena
theory
empirical
fact

unilineal cultural
  evolutionism

biological
  determinism
races

diffusion
culture traits
historical
  particularism
culture areas

functionalism
structural
  functionalism
social determinism
cultural determinism
superorganic

configurations of
  entire cultures
culture-and-
  personality school

ethnoscience
emic
etic

structuralism
French structuralism
bricolage

agency

symbolic
  anthropology
ecological
  anthropology
cultural ecology
multilineal
  evolutionism
behavioral ecology

cultural materialism
utilitarian

historical materialism

positivism
postmodernism
stopping points

ORIGINALLY, ANTHROPOLOGY AIMED to be a science of culture. Its early practitioners modeled themselves on the most successful scientists of their day—the physicists, chemists, and especially the biologists. As much as possible, they aimed to adopt the methodology of science and described their activities using scientific terminology. Thus, important late-nineteenth-century scholars like Lewis Henry Morgan and Herbert Spencer were most explicit about the fact that their work involved a search for the laws of society and culture and that discovering such laws would permit them to describe the relationships of material cause and effect that underlay social and cultural phenomena.

Since their day, the applicability of the scientific method to the study of human social and cultural life has been questioned. Although some cultural anthropologists maintain that the scientific method is appropriate to anthropology, many of their colleagues have concluded either that human cultural life is not an appropriate subject matter for "scientific" analysis or that, if it is, science itself must be reconfigured and its methodology revised in order to provide accounts of human cultural life that are not distorted beyond all recognition (also discussed in Chapter 1).

12.1 Anthropology as Science

Why did early anthropologists think that culture could be studied scientifically? If we believe E. B. Tylor, it was because culture was patterned, orderly, *lawlike*. As Tylor famously said, if law is anywhere it is everywhere. Like physical scientists and social scientists such as Herbert Spencer (1820–1903) and Emile Durkheim, Tylor and other early anthropologists believed that the phenomena of culture—languages, customs, techniques, rituals, and so forth—

*Material Phenomena → tangible + measurable
lang, cust, tech, rituals,

were **material phenomena,** phenomena that existed in the world and were tangible and measurable and could be registered by the senses. The current shape of these phenomena was the effect of other material causes at work in human society, not of metaphysical or spiritual causes. Durkheim echoed this when he later argued that social facts could be explained only by other social facts. Much of culture seemed resistant to rapid change, but when it did change, it did so in a patterned and lawlike manner. Thus, Tylor, Spencer, and Lewis Henry Morgan described culture as evolving, rather than changing unpredictably or randomly with the passage of time.

S   S   his idea

* Culture = evolving NOT changing unpredictably

In anthropology, as in science, a **theory** is a formal description of some part of the world that explains how, in terms of cause and effect, that part of the world works. Anthropology followed the lead of scientific theorizing in other fields, in which the aim was to explain a complex phenomenon by *reducing* it to a set of simpler elements whose interactions were both necessary and sufficient to produce the phenomenon in question. Because human culture in general and individual cultural traditions in particular are enormously complex phenomena, anthropologists hoped that they might discover those simpler elements and laws that *determined* the direction of cultural evolution.

theory = describes in theory how the world works in relation to cause and effect.

Early scientists, and anthropologists who wanted to imitate their method, argued that the plausibility of any theory depended on the evidence used to defend it, and they were universal in urging that only solid empirical evidence be allowed. To be **empirical** means that the evidence used to support a theory is the product of hands-on experience and can be inspected and evaluated by observers other than the original researcher. Only evidence that could meet this standard could be considered scientific **fact.** Scientific investigation has always stressed the importance of empirical research, arguing that the evidence of one's senses is a surer foundation for reliable knowledge than speculation unsupported by direct experience and that the objectivity of one's evidence must be tested against the critical observations of others before it is granted.

empirical must have evidence to support a theory - hands-on + be observed

* Must be put to the test.

thus = A FACT!

12.2 Nineteenth-Century Approaches

Nineteenth-century [unilineal cultural evolutionism] is generally regarded as the first theoretical perspective to take root in the discipline of anthropology. Evolutionary thought in nineteenth-century biology is ordinarily associated with Charles Darwin (1809–82), but cultural evolutionary thought actually predated Darwin's 1859 publication of *On the Origin of Species* and was already well developed in the work of Darwin's contemporary Herbert Spencer. Spencer thought that human societies could usefully be compared to living organisms and stressed that, over time, like living organisms, societies increased in both size and internal complexity. Spencer's ideas had parallels with the work of his contemporary, Lewis Henry Morgan. Morgan is best remembered for two key contributions to the development of anthropological theory: his emphasis on patterned variation in kinship terminologies, which led him to speculate about the different forms human families might assume in different societies, and his attempt to connect these patterns of family organization to patterns of subsistence in a universal evolutionary sequence. The sequence he proposed drew together many contemporary ideas about the evolution of culture, including the idea that all cultures everywhere either had evolved or would evolve through the same sequence of stages: Savagery, Barbarism, and Civilization (also discussed in Chapter 8).

Morgan recognized that his scheme was tentative in places and required more evidence to sustain certain claims. Nevertheless, like other cultural evolutionists in this period, he was convinced that he had discovered underlying laws of cultural change and that better empirical evidence collected by future researchers would refine the patterns he had exposed.

In a scientific world where researchers hope to reduce complex effects to simple causes, theories of cultural evolution were challenged by other theories that claimed to explain the diversity of human social life in different ways. One of the strongest competitors in the late nineteenth century was the argument that biological differences between different human populations explained their different ways of life or, put another way, that a group's way

(c) biological determination → scientific racism, people act differently bc/ of their innate biological makeup.

of life was determined by its distinct, innate biological makeup. This approach, called **biological determinism,** is also known as *scientific racism,* for it claimed to have empirical evidence that supported both the existence of biologically distinct human populations, or **races,** and the relative rankings of these races on a scale of superiority and inferiority. Not surprisingly, this Eurocentric framework assumed that light-skinned European races were superior to darker-skinned African or Asian or Native American races, since the latter had been conquered and dominated by the former.

(c) racial framework

Late-nineteenth-century evolutionary anthropologists never fully separated themselves from the biological determinists. Even though their defense of a universal set of cultural evolutionary stages presupposed a common humanity and common destiny shared by all the peoples of the world (which they sometimes described as the *psychic unity of mankind*), they believed that this common potentiality had not been equally developed in all living human populations and that its actual degree of realization was indicated by the stage of cultural evolution a particular society had achieved. Thus, although the descendants of people whose way of life was classified as "savage" might one day achieve the same level of sophistication as a contemporary people classified as "barbarian," there was no question of considering them equal at the present time. People living at a more highly evolved level of culture were simply viewed as more highly evolved *people* than those living at lower levels. Not until the twentieth century and the work of North American anthropologists like Franz Boas and his students would scientific racism be rejected as an explanation of human cultural diversity (also discussed in Chapter 2).

(s) even today higher evolved = better

(c) Boas rejected explanation of human cultural diversity.

12.3 Early-Twentieth-Century Approaches

Although unilineal evolutionary schemes were built on valid observations about changes in human subsistence strategies and incorporated empirical evidence about kinship that has proved reliable over time, these schemes also included (as all scientific theories do) considerable speculation. As the twentieth century

handwritten: ✱ diffusion → borrowing of cultural features

began, German anthropologists were offering a very different universal theory of culture change, based on the supposedly regular spread of various cultural items from group to group by **diffusion,** or borrowing. Some proponents of both views were becoming increasingly extreme in their claims. In the face of this extremism, Boas in the United States denounced both theories. In the best scientific fashion, he used empirical ethnographic and historical evidence to expose the inadequacies of both forms of reductionism. Boas agreed that cultures changed over time, but such change could not be confined to passage through a single sequence of progressive evolutionary stages. Rather, historical evidence showed that cultures sometimes simplified over time, instead of becoming more complex, and in any case could easily skip stages by borrowing advanced cultural inventions from their neighbors. Similarly, although cultures are full of cultural items or activities, called **culture traits,** borrowed from neighboring societies, anthropologists go too far if they assume that most human groups are incapable of inventing anything on their own and must await the innovations that spread from a few favored sites of cultural creativity. Boas pointed out that some social problems—how to organize kinship, for example—have only a few possible solutions and are likely to be independently discovered again and again by widely separated peoples.

handwritten left margin: © Boas - cultures do evolve but don't have set perameters

handwritten right margin: ✱ ✓ Culture traits - items or activities related - a culture

Boas and his students rejected both extreme evolutionary schemes and extreme diffusion schemes, preferring to focus on the distinct histories of change in particular human societies, an approach that came to be called **historical particularism.** By comparing the culture histories of neighboring peoples, they were able to trace the limits of diffusion of many cultural traits, eventually producing maps of **culture areas** far smaller and more complex than the vast maps of the German diffusionists.

handwritten left margin: historical particularism = change in a particular human society

handwritten right margin: culture areas far smaller, more complex

The theoretical extremism that Boas rejected was also rejected in England and France at about the same time. Although not ruling out the possibility of one day being able to construct a theory of cultural evolution, anthropologists like Bronislaw Malinowski and A. R. Radcliffe-Brown (1881–1955) in England and sociologist/anthropologist Emile Durkheim and his colleagues in France declared a moratorium on speculations about cultural evolution unsupported by empirical evidence. All urged that research focus instead on living societies in order to collect precisely the kind of detailed empirical evidence that might one day enable the construction of a plausible theory of cultural evolution.

Malinowski set an example with his own field research in the Trobriand Islands. Not only was he a pioneer in modern participant-observation field methods, but he also set standards for the collection of ethnographic data that had a lasting influence on subsequent generations of anthropologists. His approach was to classify the customs and beliefs he learned about in the field in terms of the function each one performed in the satisfaction of what he called *basic human needs* (also discussed in Chapter 8). For this reason, his research program became known as **function-alism.** Malinowski's main goal in much of his ethnographic writing was to debunk contemporary stereotypes of "savage" peoples as irrational, compulsive slaves to their passions, and so he emphasized repeatedly how orderly and well organized Trobriand life was and how customs that appeared irrational to ignorant outsiders could actually be shown to play important functions in meeting the Trobriand Islanders' basic human needs.

The theoretical response of other British and French anthropologists was to focus not on the function of particular customs in meeting the needs of individual human beings but rather on their function in preserving the structure of the society itself. Hence, this school of thought came to be called **structural functionalism.** Heavily influenced by the writings of Durkheim, Radcliffe-Brown was its most tireless promoter in Britain. Structural-functionalists were concerned with what kept societies from falling apart (discussed in Chapter 7), and they were able to demonstrate that a variety of social practices described by ethnographers—witchcraft accusations, kinship organization, myths, and the like—performed this function.

In the mid-twentieth century, an antagonism developed between structural-functionalist British social anthropologists (as they called themselves) and North American cultural anthropologists. In retrospect, the antagonism seems rather trivial, but for many anthropologists at the time, the issue was whether anthropology would be taken seriously as a science. As we have seen, British social anthropologists, via Radcliffe-Brown, who was influenced by Durkheim, took *society* as their defining concept. To them, human bodies arranged in space in particular configurations constituted the unquestionable reality that must be shaped by material laws of cause and effect operating in the social realm. North American anthropologists, however, focused on the concept of *culture*—the ideas, beliefs, values, and meanings that different groups of people developed to express their understanding of their lives and themselves.

For a British social anthropologist, nothing could be less material, and thus possess less causal power, than ideas, beliefs, and values. For the most outspoken of them, culture was a by-product, or a rationalization of material social arrangements that had nothing to do with culture but were instead the inevitable outcome of the operation of universal social laws (the necessity of maintaining social solidarity so that the social group endures over time) that automatically forced living human organisms into particular social configurations in particular circumstances. But North American cultural anthropologists countered such arguments by emphasizing the power of culture to shape all aspects of peoples' lives, including the ways they organized their societies.

To counter the **social determinism** advocated by some structural-functionalists, some cultural anthropologists proposed a form of **cultural determinism**. For example, A. L. Kroeber (1876–1960), one of Boas's students, argued that culture was a **superorganic** phenomenon (to be contrasted with inorganic matter and organic life). That is, although culture was carried by organic human beings, it existed in an impersonal realm apart from them, evolving according to its own internal laws, unaffected by laws governing nonliving matter or the evolution of living organisms, and essentially beyond the control of human beings whom it molded and on whom, in a sense, it was parasitic. The views of social determinists and cultural determinists were so extreme, in part because they completely rejected any explanation of society or culture that would locate its origins either outside human individuals in some unseen, immaterial, personalized force like God or within human individuals in the psychological structure of their minds. Durkheim, Radcliffe-Brown, and Kroeber, each in his own way, struggled to defend the view that sociocultural beliefs and practices constituted a distinct scientific subject matter that had to be explained in its own terms by specialists who understood how it operated—that is, by social (or cultural) scientists like themselves.

In North America, cultural anthropologists developed a series of theoretical perspectives based on their conviction that culture shaped human behavior, including the construction of particular forms of social structure. In the early twentieth century, inspired by the work of Ruth Benedict, they turned to psychology and attempted to apply what was understood about the configuration of individual human personalities to the **configurations of entire cultures.** Attempts to explain why adults from different cultures held different values and engaged in different practices promoted attention on child-rearing practices, leading to the development of the **culture-and-personality school,** to which Margaret Mead was a major contributor (also discussed in Chapter 4).

12.4 Mid-Twentieth-Century Approaches

Developments in the study of language inspired other cultural anthropologists to borrow insights from linguistics in attempting to explain how culture worked. One outcome of this was the development of **ethnoscience,** a movement in cultural anthropology that involved borrowing the techniques perfected by descriptive linguists to elicit information about culturally relevant domains of meaning by studying how the members of a particular group classified objects and events in their environments. Ethnoscientists were extremely concerned that the taxonomies they elicited not be contaminated by the imposition of their own cultural perspectives. Therefore, they went to great pains to preserve the boundary between the culturally relevant categories of their informants, called **emic** categories, and the categories that were the product of anthropological theory, called **etic** categories (also discussed in Chapter 3).

Another rather different attempt to apply insights from linguistics to cultural analysis was developed by French anthropologist Claude Lévi-Strauss. Inspired by the so-called structural linguistics of Swiss scholar Ferdinand de Saussure (1857–1913, see Chapter 3), particularly its analysis of phonemic structures, Lévi-Strauss tried to see whether the same kinds of structural patterns might be found in other domains of culture. Lévi-Strauss first applied his structural analysis—later called **structuralism** or **French structuralism**—to the study of kinship systems, but he gained an international reputation both inside and outside anthropology for his structural studies of myth (myth is discussed in Chapter 5).

Lévi-Strauss collected multiple variants of numerous myths from indigenous societies in the Americas and appeared to be, on the surface at least, as interested in explaining cultural diversity as other contemporary cultural anthropologists. But he parted company with those anthropologists, such as ethnoscientists, who used linguistic methods to produce more detailed and accurate descriptions of culture but who still thought of culture as a historically contingent set of learned beliefs and practices. Instead, Lévi-Strauss saw surface diversity as the by-product of much simpler underlying processes of thought rooted in the structure of the human mind itself. Lévi-Strauss argued that, because all human beings were members of the same species, they possessed the same innate mental structures. The most obvious of these structures, he asserted, was the tendency to classify phenomena in terms of binary oppositions, like male-female, night-day, up-down, or mind-body. Lévi-Strauss argued that the diversity of cultural phenomena around the world was a surface diversity, the output produced by people with identical mental structures who were working with different kinds of natural and cultural resources. All people thus were engaged in a kind of cultural tinkering, what he called **bricolage,** in which they combined and contrasted elements of their experience in complex constructions rooted in a universal set of human mental structures.

Structuralism was immensely influential inside as well as outside anthropology. Literary critics, in particular, seized upon structuralism as a theoretical toolkit that could help them dissect the structure of literary or artistic work. But Lévi-Strauss and other structuralists also had their critics. Early criticism mostly concerned the validity of particular structural analyses of myths or other cultural phenomena. Different analysts, using what they thought were the same structuralist methods, frequently produced different analyses of the same cultural materials, leading critics to raise the question of just how "scientific" structural analysis actually was and how much it depended on the analysts' own interpretive style.

Later criticisms, which fed into postmodernism, pointed out that structuralists (not unlike the Chomskyan linguists mentioned in Chapter 3) assume that cultures are monolithic and that cultural products, like myths, can have only a single "correct" reading. Structuralists wanted their readings accepted as objectively valid, like scientific discoveries, but their critics argued that the attempt to reduce all the variants of a myth to a single underlying structure ignored the possibility that the variants themselves contained important information about the social, political, or historical self-understanding of the myth-tellers. Rather than simply being the vehicles through which myths worked themselves out across time and space, perhaps the members of each society who recounted the myth were agents attempting to use the resources of myth to make sense of specific concrete social experiences. By reducing all cultural forms to the innate structures of the human mind, structuralism appeared to some observers to be merely a new kind of biological determinism.

Structuralism is only one of a series of theoretical perspectives in contemporary cultural anthropology that have come under fire because of their apparent denial of human agency (defined in Chapter 4). An ongoing struggle in anthropology concerns the relationship of culture to the individual (discussed in Chapter 4). While most contemporary parties to the struggle agree that culture is learned, they disagree concerning how much is learned, how important it is for human survival, and how far individuals can go in modifying or rejecting aspects of their cultural heritage.

A different and very influential approach to human action developed in anthropology in the 1960s. This is referred to as **symbolic anthropology,** or sometimes *interpretive anthropology,* because of its emphasis on systems of meanings rather than on innate structures of mind or on the material dimensions of human life. For symbolic anthropologists, human culture is a system of symbols and meanings that human beings create themselves and then use to direct, organize, and give coherence to their lives. The most prominent symbolic anthropologists of the last part of the twentieth century were Mary Douglas, Victor Turner, and Clifford Geertz.

The work of Mary Douglas (1921–) combines a commitment to Durkheimian functionalism with an emphasis on the ways in which cultural symbols both reflect and shore up particular social orders. In her most famous book, *Purity and Danger* (1966), she explored widespread beliefs about purity and pollution in different societies, arguing that pollution was best understood as "matter out of place" within a particular symbolic order. Douglas drew attention to the ways in which a particular society's ideas about purity and pollution were regularly based on a metaphoric connection between the human body and society. She argued, for example, that symbolic practices that appeared to be concerned with protecting vulnerable human bodies from pollution were actually concerned with keeping vulnerable social structures from falling apart. Social vulnerabilities were symbolically represented as bodily vulnerabilities, as when the orifices of the body were seen to stand for points of entry into or exit from the body politic. Thus, food taboos designed to protect individual bodies from ingesting polluting substances could be understood as a symbolic way of protecting a vulnerable social order from dangerous outside forces. Douglas's work focuses on forms of symbolism that appear to be universal in human cultures, an emphasis that sets her apart from both Turner and Geertz, who both paid far more attention to the particular symbolic practices of specific societies.

Victor Turner (1920–83) was trained as a structural function-alist in England but became dissatisfied with examining abstract social structure. Rather than emphasizing people's unthinking conformity to the underlying principles that ordered their society, Turner's work emphasized practice and performance. His work came to focus on *social dramas:* people's concrete interactions and conflicts in everyday social life. Turner showed how social dramas not only offered anthropologists insight into the structure of a given society but also revealed how people in that society made sense of their lives. Turner's interest in social dramas led him into studies of ritual (see Chapter 5), pilgrimage, and theater. In all of these studies, he was concerned with how the symbols of a par-ticular group of people—those "things that stand for other things"—were used as stores of meaning and as resources for social action. For Turner, what mattered were not the symbols themselves but what they meant to specific people and how they led to action in specific social situations.

Like Turner, Clifford Geertz (1926–) has also been interested in symbols and their interpretation. For Geertz, culture is a system of symbols and meanings that are publicly displayed in objects and actions. Drawing on literary theory more than on drama the-ory, Geertz came to see cultures as made up of *texts,* "stories that people tell themselves about themselves." In his view, the anthro-pologist's job is to learn to read those texts, not the way natives did, since it was impossible to get inside the natives' heads, but from within the same cultural context. Geertz proposed the phrase *thick description* for this process of finding the local mean-ings of cultural texts and in so doing drew attention to the fact that written texts were the typical product of ethnographic field-work. Beginning in the early 1970s, many anthropologists in-creasingly came to see that their task was to *write about* other societies, not merely to collect and analyze data, and that their ethnographies should be understood as texts to be read alongside the natives' own texts.

Both Geertz and Turner were influential outside of anthropol-ogy as well, in such branches of the humanities as religious studies

*Geertz
- read
+ learn
about
culture
Changing
to literary
Critisism*

and literary theory. Indeed, a common complaint about Geertz's work was that by relying so heavily on the interpretive skills of the anthropologist, it made the field more like literary criticism than social science.

The mid-twentieth century also saw a revival of evolutionary thinking in North American cultural anthropology. The new evolutionary anthropology rejected biological determinism, together with the racist evolutionary scheme that went with it. At the same time, evolutionary anthropologists accepted current biological theories of evolution by natural selection and argued that human biological evolution, like the biological evolution of all organisms, involved adaptation to the environment. If varying modes of human adaptation were not the outcome of variations in human biology, some anthropologists reasoned, then perhaps the environments themselves were responsible for human cultural diversity. Anthropologists who ask such questions today usually are described as doing one or another kind of **ecological anthropology** (see Chapter 8).

*ecological
anthro.
↓
environ.
responsable
for
human
cultural
diversity*

Ecologists and ecologically inclined anthropologists generally analyze particular human populations as parts of *ecosystems*; that is, they are one group of living organisms that, together with other organisms, make their living within a given environmental setting. This setting is called a *system* because it exhibits a balance in terms of the variety and size of different populations and the resources they depend upon to survive and reproduce. This balance is usually described in terms of a patterned flow and exchange of energy. Stable ecosystems are ones in which each population occupies its own *niche*; that is, all coresident populations make their livings in different ways and do not compete with one another.

An important founder of ecological approaches in cultural anthropology was Julian Steward (1902–72). His analytic framework, which is called **cultural ecology,** studied the ways in which specific human cultures interacted with their environment. Steward was an evolutionary thinker: He argued that cultural change over time was conditioned by the specific kinds of cultural devel-

*Cultural ecology → spec. human cultures
interacted w/ environment*

opments, particularly in subsistence technology, available in a given society and the ways in which members of that culture used their technology to obtain what they needed to survive from the particular environment in which they lived. As cultural systems changed the way they interacted with their environments, thus changing their adaptations, they evolved to new levels of sociocultural integration.

Steward did not believe in the universal stages of cultural evolution supported by his contemporary Leslie White (1900–75). For White, cultural evolution was a general process encompassing all the cultures of humanity. White recast the major stages of cultural evolution proposed by nineteenth-century anthropologists (and by Karl Marx) in terms of how much energy per capita per year was captured by particular cultural systems. For White, cultures evolved as they captured more energy or as their technologies improved, or both. Using these criteria, White identified three major evolutionary turning points: (1) the domestication of plants and animals (the agricultural revolution of antiquity), (2) the beginnings of mechanization (linked to the "fuel revolution" at the beginning of the nineteenth century), and (3) the technological harnessing of atomic energy in the mid-twentieth century. Steward's approach to cultural evolution, by contrast, has been described as multilineal evolutionism. Steward focused not on global evolutionary trends but rather on particular sequences of culture change, showing how local, evolutionary trajectories in similar societies could go in different directions, depending on the society's overall culture, its technology, and the particular environment to which each society was adapting. Today, those evolutionary anthropologists who assign symbolic culture a key role in their explanations of human adaptations to their environments (e.g., cultural inheritance theorists) are sometimes said to be continuing the practices of cultural ecology and multilineal evolutionism pioneered by Steward.

Research in ecological anthropology addresses debates about human agency because some ecological anthropologists argue that human adaptations are heavily circumscribed by environmental restrictions. In common with sociobiology, for example, **behav-ioral ecology** applies to human societies the same analytic princi-ples that have been used to study the social behavior of animals, especially the social insects (e.g., ants). Indeed, sociobiology-inspired behavioral ecological anthropologists claim that, over the millennia, natural selection operating on individuals in particular environments not only has selected for genes responsible for the physical and behavioral traits of *individuals* but also has operated to increase the frequency in individuals of genes that control our *social* behavior.

Behavioral ecologists thus argue that we have been pro-grammed to respond to others in stereotypical (but individually adaptive) ways that neither cultural conditioning nor individual willpower can modify. Put another way, behavioral ecology stresses that natural selection has produced human beings pro-grammed to automatically find ways of maximizing their own individual self-interest, which in evolutionary terms means get-ting as many of one's genes into the next generation as possible (see Chapter 8). Behavioral ecology has little or no role for sym-bolic culture in its accounts of human adaptation, because act-ing in terms of arbitrary symbol systems could potentially mislead individuals into acting in ways that go against their own self-interest, such as taking risks for others with no obvious gain for oneself (or one's genes). If such evolutionary programming is as extensive as some behavioral ecological anthropologists claim, it would appear to restrict human agency just as much as the kinds of biological programming claimed by the biological determinists.

By drawing attention to ecological factors that affect cultural adaptations, ecological anthropologists have attempted to show the inadequacies of cultural theories that take no account of the material conditions of human life. Two other theoretical move-ments in the latter half of the twentieth century, each rather differ-ent from the ecological approaches described previously, also tried to argue for theories of culture that take the material world into account.

One such attempt has been the **cultural materialism** of Marvin Harris (1927–2001), a theoretical perspective rooted in Harris's idiosyncratic readings of Marx, Engels, White, and Steward. He tries to tame what he sees as the extravagant claims of cultural determinists by pointing out the material constraints with which any cultural adaptation must come to terms. He attempts to show that particular customs that shock or disgust us today, such as warfare, cannibalism, or infanticide, were invented to ensure human survival in some past habitat. Although these are cultural inventions, their inventors are no more conscious of why they are doing what they do than are the human beings described by behavioral ecologists. In both cases, moreover, the same kinds of self-interest calculations are said to govern the selection of particular practices. Indeed, both behavioral ecology and cultural materialism take an essentially **utilitarian** approach to the explanation of the evolution of cultural diversity: in any given case, behaviors are selected because they confer the greatest good, either for a particular individual (behavioral ecology) or for the group (cultural materialism).

The other brand of materialism that has been influential in recent cultural anthropology is the **historical materialism** based on the writings of Karl Marx and his followers. The main feature distinguishing Harris's cultural materialism from Marxian historical materialism is the role of the material forces of history. Whereas Harris's approach explains cultural adaptation or evolution in terms of local conditions, the Marxian approach explains cultural evolution in world-historical terms; after all, Marx was another nineteenth-century unilineal evolutionist. But the ways in which he differed from other unilineal evolutionists made him an inspiration for anthropologists dissatisfied with accounts of culture change that did not take into account social and political conflict, domination, and inequality (discussed in Chapters 7, 8, and 11). Marx attributed large-scale sociocultural change to the working out of material contradictions within the organization of society (its relations of production). Ecological constraints are less important than the social constraints and contradictions generated by a particular, culturally constructed mode of production (e.g., between landowners and the people who own no land and so must rent from the owner). Marxian ideas were also attractive because, in at least some of his writings, Marx suggested that human beings could exercise agency—could "make history"— albeit not under conditions of their own choosing. The material constraints of history limited the action they could take, limited even the alternatives they could imagine to the present order, but did not necessarily turn them into puppets unable to affect their cultural surroundings. Although the political hopes inspired by historical materialism have dimmed considerably with the end of the Cold War, Marx's crucial insights into the workings of capitalism and the mechanisms of domination continue to offer theoretical inspiration to some anthropologists.

12.5 Contemporary Debates

At the beginning of the twentieth century, cultural anthropologists wanted to create a science of culture. At the beginning of the twenty-first century, cultural anthropology has split into two camps divided not only over whether a science of culture is possible but also over whether science itself, as traditionally conceived, is possible. One camp consists of those who defend the traditional understanding of science, which many call **positivism** (see Chapter 1). They are committed to the view that universal, objective truth can be discovered by rational methods, that scientific explanations involve reducing complex effects to their simpler determining causes, and that these procedures ultimately will unify knowledge from all domains of experience in one grand "theory of everything."

The other camp takes very seriously the critique of modern science embodied in **postmodernism.** Its members regard the universalizing, reductionist approach of positivist science as inadequate and distorting when applied to the study of culture. For them, taking symbolic culture seriously requires a reflexive, interpretive approach in which the details of specific cultural realities are not eliminated, in which people's individual voices and their

TABLE 12.1   Key Theoretical Positions in Anthropology

LATE NINETEENTH CENTURY	FIRST HALF OF TWENTIETH CENTURY	MID-TWENTIETH CENTURY	LATE TWENTIETH CENTURY
Unilineal evolution	Historical particularism	Ethnoscience	Symbolic anthropology
Diffusion	Functionalism	Structuralism	Behavioral ecology
	Structural functionalism	Ecological anthropology	Cultural materialism
	Cultural determinism	Cultural ecology	Postmodernism
	Culture-and-personality approach	Multilineal evolutionism	

unique understandings are not silenced by generalizations. They call into question the supposed universal truths of "scientific anthropology." (Table 12.1 lists the key theoretical positions in anthropology.)

Since the late 1980s and early 1990s, many anthropologists have realized that, for all their political attractiveness, extremist positions are unsatisfactory. The issues are complex, however, because some kinds of progressive politics, such as the condemnation of genocide, seem to rest squarely on the assumption that all human beings everywhere are bearers of universal human rights that *nobody* can be permitted to ignore. It is precisely in the area of human rights that the critics of interpretivism have made their most powerful argument. If all action is culturally relative, they argue, then one has no grounds for international condemnation of leaders of nation-states who persecute their own citizens. If post-modernists have their way, they conclude, and all forms of culture are assumed to be equally valuable, then the grounds for moral outrage at genocide evaporate. Indeed, the leaders of genocide campaigns frequently attempt to silence international critics by defending their actions as culturally appropriate for their societies, and they accuse their critics of ethnocentrism or imperialism. Some cultural anthropologists are quite open about what have been called the **stopping points** beyond which their analysis cannot go. For those of a traditional positivist bent, it may be deterministic theories that attempt to construct scientific bases for racism or sexism or other forms of social inequality. For those of an interpretivist bent, it may be forms of relativism that would explain away, say, poverty or violence against women.

The most courageous and interesting work is being done by those who try to walk a very fine line between the extremes of determinism (whether biological, cultural, ecological, or historical) and the extremes of relativism. Because there are no clear guidelines for how to do this successfully, at present one encounters a variety of experiments in fieldwork, in theory, and in the work of combining them in written ethnography. One of the most exciting of these developments involves the attempt to reexamine the ways in which knowledge is produced in different scholarly disciplines, including anthropology, and by different kinds of researchers, be they "positivists" or "interpretivists" or something in between. One of the reasons why many contemporary anthropologists insist on walking the narrow line between positivism and interpretivism is that they realize that there is no simple relation between a particular set of knowledge claims and a particular political agenda. Claiming that women are "natural peacemakers," for example, might be a justification for placing women in high political office but has more often been used (at least in the West) as a justification for keeping women outside of politics because of their supposed incapacity to make war. Responsible scholarship (as well as responsible politics) thus requires paying more attention to what Donna Haraway calls the "situated knowledges" produced by differently oriented observers engaged in different forms of knowledge production.

This approach builds on the insights that emerged when cultural anthropologists began to pay attention to the reflexive dimension of fieldwork and recognized that making clear the historical, social, cultural, political, and economic contexts within which scholarly research is conducted can actually *increase,* rather than decrease, our ability to recognize where a particular set of knowledge claims are strongest and where they are weakest. Thus, Ethnographer A's observations about the culture of the X people may be an extremely accurate reflection not of the views of all members of the society but only of elite males, since young people and women did not talk to Ethnographer A. Similarly, claims about the causes for patterned social behavior in a termite nest may be very strong in the context of research on social insects but very weak in its attempt to invoke the same causes to explain patterned social behavior in human societies. It is not necessary to dismiss either Ethnographer A or biological science as totally false simply because some of the knowledge claims made by some scholars fail to explain crucial features of human social and cultural life.

This same approach has also led anthropologists to question the assumption that anthropological categories—ritual or kinship, for examples—are timeless, universal structures that are not dependent on historical contingencies for the ways in which they are expressed among specific groups of people. The strengths of much recent work in cultural anthropology lie in continuing commitment to ethnographic particularities that frequently resist assimilation into predictable theoretical categories. Much contemporary ethnography relates macro processes of globalization with the micro level of specific people's everyday life. This work, cultural anthropologists often discover, calls into question both positivist and postmodern positions because it focuses on the often unpredictable ways people come to terms with these forces as they construct meanings in the historical and cultural contexts of their own changing lives. This enduring commitment to recognizing the reality of other perspectives and taking them seriously keeps cultural anthropology a vibrant, exciting, and compelling discipline with great potential for allowing human beings to come to know and understand themselves better.

For Further Reading

THEORY

Bernard 2000; Geertz 1973; Knauft 1996; Kuper 1996; McGee and Warms 1996; Moore 1997; Rosaldo 1989

Bibliography

Abu-Lughod, Janet. *Before European Hegemony: The World System A.D. 1250–1350.* New York: Oxford University Press, 1989.

Agar, Michael. *Language Shock: Understanding the Culture of Conversation.* New York: Morrow, 1994.

———. *The Professional Stranger.* 2d ed. San Diego: Academic Press, 1996.

Akmajian, Adrian et al. *Linguistics: An Introduction to Language and Communication.* 4th ed. Cambridge, MA: MIT Press, 2001.

Anderson, Benedict. *Imagined Communities.* London: Verso, 1983.

Appadurai, Arjun. *Modernity at Large: Cultural Dimensions of Globalization.* Minneapolis: University of Minnesota Press, 1996.

Arens, W., and Ivan Karp. *Creativity of Power: Cosmology and Action in African Societies.* Washington, DC: Smithsonian Institution Press, 1989.

Ashmore, Wendy, and Robert Sharer. *Discovering Our Past: A Brief Introduction to Archaeology.* 3d ed. Mountain View, CA: Mayfield, 2000.

Barnouw, Victor. *Culture and Personality.* 4th ed. Homewood, IL: Dorsey, 1985.

Behar, Ruth. *The Vulnerable Observer.* Boston: Beacon Press, 1997.

Bernard, Alan. *History and Theory in Anthropology.* New York: Cambridge University Press, 2000.

Bernard, H. Russell. *Research Methods in Anthropology.* 2d ed. Thousand Oaks, CA: Sage, 1994.

Blackwood, Evelyn, and Saskia E. Wieringa, eds. *Female Desires: Same-Sex Relations and Transgender Practices across Cultures.* New York: Columbia University Press, 1999.

223

Bock, Philip K., ed. *Psychological Anthropology.* Westport, CT: Praeger, 1994.

Blount, Ben G., ed. *Language, Culture, and Society: A Book of Readings.* 2d ed. Prospect Heights, IL: Waveland Press, 1995.

Bohannan, Paul. *How Culture Works.* New York: Free Press, 1995.

Bonvillain, Nancy. *Language, Culture, and Communication: The Meaning of Messages.* Englewood Cliffs, NJ: Prentice-Hall, 1993.

———. *Women and Men: Cultural Constructions of Gender.* Englewood Cliffs, NJ: Prentice-Hall, 1995.

Bowen, John, ed. *Religions in Practice: An Approach to the Anthropology of Religion.* Needham Heights, MA: Allyn & Bacon, 1998a.

———. *Religion in Culture and Society.* Needham Heights, MA: Allyn & Bacon, 1998b.

Bradburd, Daniel. *Being There: The Necessity of Fieldwork.* Washington, DC: Smithsonian Institution Press, 1998.

Brenneis, Donald, and Ronald Macaulay, eds. *The Matrix of Language: Contemporary Linguistic Anthropology.* Boulder, CO: Westview Press, 1996.

Child, Alice B., and Irvin L. Child. *Religion and Magic in the Life of Traditional Peoples.* Englewood Cliffs, NJ: Prentice-Hall, 1993.

Clifford, James. *The Predicament of Culture.* Cambridge, MA: Harvard University Press, 1988.

Coe, Sophie, and Michael Coe. *The True History of Chocolate.* London: Thames & Hudson, 1996.

Cole, Michael, and Sylvia Scribner. *Culture and Thought: A Psychological Introduction.* New York: Wiley, 1974.

Collier, Jane Fishburne, and Sylvia Junko Yanigasako, eds. *Gender and Kinship.* Stanford, CA: Stanford University Press, 1987.

Colloredo-Mansfeld, Rudi. *The Native Leisure Class: Consumption and Cultural Creativity in the Andes.* Chicago: University of Chicago Press, 1999.

Contemporary Issues Forum: Race and Racism. *American Anthropologist* 100(3), 1998.

Daniel, E. Valentine, and John Knudsen, eds. *Mistrusting Refugees.* Berkeley: University of California Press, 1995.

Di Leonardo, Micaela, ed. *Gender at the Crossroads of Knowledge: Feminist Anthropology in the Postmodern Era.* Berkeley: University of California Press, 1991.

Doi, Takeo. *The Anatomy of Self.* Tokyo: Kodansha International, 1985.

Duranti, Alessandro. *Linguistic Anthropology.* Cambridge: Cambridge University Press, 1997.

Featherstone, Mike, ed. *Global Culture: Nationalism, Globalization, and Modernity.* London: Sage, 1990.

Fiddis, Nick. *Meat: A Natural Symbol.* London: Routledge, 1991.

Fried, M. H. *The Evolution of Political Society.* New York: Random House, 1967.

Gamst, F. C., and E. Norbeck, eds. *Ideas of Culture.* New York: Holt, Rinehart & Winston, 1976.

Gardner, Katy, and David Lewis. *Anthropology, Development and the Post-Modern Challenge.* London: Pluto Press, 1996.

Geertz, Clifford. *The Interpretation of Cultures.* New York: Basic Books, 1973.

Ginsburg, Faye, and Rayna Rapp. *Conceiving the New World Order: The Global Politics of Reproduction.* Berkeley: University of California Press, 1995.

Goody, Jack, and Stanley Tambiah. *Bridewealth and Dowry.* Cambridge: Cambridge University Press, 1973.

Graburn, Nelson, ed. *Readings in Kinship and Social Structure.* New York: Harper & Row, 1971.

Gudeman, Stephen. *Economics as Culture: Models and Metaphors of Livelihood.* London: Routledge & Kegan Paul, 1986.

Gutmann, Matthew. "Trafficking in Men: The Anthropology of Masculinity." *Annual Review of Anthropology* 26 (1997): 385–409.

Halperin, Rhoda H. *Cultural Economies: Past and Present.* Austin: University of Texas Press, 1994.

Hannerz, Ulf. *Transnational Connections: Culture, People, Places.* London: Routledge, 1996.

Harris, Olivia, ed. *Inside and Outside the Law: Anthropological Studies of Authority and Ambiguity.* New York: Routledge, 1997.

Herdt, Gilbert, ed. *Third Sex, Third Gender: Beyond Sexual Dimorphism in Culture and History.* New York: Zone Books, 1994.

Hicks, David, ed. *Religion and Belief: Readings in the Anthropology of Religion.* New York: McGraw-Hill College, 1999.

Hill, Jane, and Judith Irvine, eds. *Responsibility and Evidence in Oral Discourse.* Cambridge: Cambridge University Press, 1992.

Hughey, Michael. *New Tribalisms: The Resurgence of Race and Ethnicity.* New York: New York University Press, 1998.

Ingham, John M. *Psychological Anthropology Reconsidered.* Cambridge: Cambridge University Press, 1996.

Kakar, Sudhir. *The Inner World*. 2d ed. New York: Oxford University Press, 1981.

Kearney, Michael. "The Local and the Global: The Anthropology of Globalization and Transnationalism." *Annual Review of Anthropology* 24 (1995): 547–65.

———. *Reconceptualizing the Peasantry: Anthropology in Global Perspective*. Boulder, CO: Westview Press, 1996.

Klass, Morton. *Ordered Universes: Approaches to the Anthropology of Religion*. Boulder, CO: Westview Press, 1995.

Knauft, Bruce. *Genealogies for the Present in Cultural Anthropology*. New York: Routledge, 1996.

Kuper, Adam. *Anthropology and Anthropologists: The Modern British School*. 3d ed. London: Routledge, 1996.

Lambek, Michael, ed. *A Reader in the Anthropology of Religion*. Malden, MA: Blackwell Publishers, 2002.

Lave, Jean. *Cognition in Practice*. Cambridge: Cambridge University Press, 1988.

Lehman, Arthur, and James Myers, eds. *Magic, Witchcraft, and Religion: An Anthropological Study of the Supernatural*. 4th ed. Mountain View, CA: Mayfield, 1996.

Levine, Nancy. *The Dynamics of Polyandry: Kinship, Domesticity, and Population on the Tibetan Border*. Chicago: University of Chicago Press, 1988.

Lewellen, Ted C. *Political Anthropology*. 2d ed. South Hadley, MA: Bergin & Garvey, 1992.

———. *Dependency and Development*. Westport, CT: Bergin & Garvey, 1995.

Littlefield, Alice, and Hill Gates, eds. *Marxist Approaches in Economic Anthropology*. Lanham, MD: University Press of America and Society for Economic Anthropology, 1991.

Lutz, Catherine A. *Unnatural Emotions: Everyday Sentiments on a Micronesian Atoll and Their Challenge to Western Theory*. Cambridge: Cambridge University Press, 1988.

Malkki, Liisa H. "Refugees and Exile: From 'Refugee Status' to the National Order of Things." *Annual Review of Anthropology* 24 (1995): 495–523.

Marcus, George, and Michael Fischer. *Anthropology as Cultural Critique: An Experimental Moment in the Human Sciences*. Chicago: University of Chicago Press, 1986.

McGee, R. Jon, and Richard Warms. *Anthropological Theory: An Introductory History*. Mountain View, CA: Mayfield, 1996.

Messer, Ellen. "Anthropology and Human Rights." *Annual Review of Anthropology* 22 (1993): 221–49.

Miller, Barbara Diane, ed. *Sex and Gender Hierarchies.* Cambridge: Cambridge University Press, 1993.

Mintz, Sidney W. *Sweetness and Power: The Place of Sugar in Modern History.* New York: Penguin Books, 1985.

———. *Tasting Food, Tasting Freedom: Excursions into Eating, Culture, and the Past.* Boston: Beacon Press, 1996.

Moore, Jerry D. *Visions of Culture: An Introduction to Anthropological Theories and Theorists.* Walnut Creek, CA: AltaMira Press, 1997.

Nader, Laura. *Law in Culture and Society.* Berkeley: University of California Press, 1997.

Nagengast, Carole. "Violence, Terror, and the Crisis of the State." *Annual Review of Anthropology* 23 (1994): 109–36.

Netting, Robert. *Smallholders, Householders: Farm Families and the Ecology of Intensive, Sustainable Agriculture.* Stanford, CA: Stanford University Press, 1993.

Netting, Robert, Richard Wilk, and E. J. Arnould, eds. *Households: Comparative and Historical Studies of the Domestic Group.* Berkeley: University of California Press, 1984.

Park, Michael. *Biological Anthropology.* 2d ed. Mountain View, CA: Mayfield, 1998.

Parkin, Robert. *Kinship: An Introduction to Basic Concepts.* Oxford: Blackwell, 1997.

Peletz, Michael. "Kinship Studies in Late Twentieth-Century Anthropology." *Annual Review of Anthropology* 24 (1995): 343–72.

Pels, Peter. "The Anthropology of Colonialism: Culture, History, and the Emergence of Western Governmentality." *Annual Review of Anthropology* 26 (1997): 163–83.

Plattner, Stuart, ed. *Economic Anthropology.* Stanford, CA: Stanford University Press, 1989.

Pospisil, Leonard. *Anthropology of Law: A Comparative Theory.* New York: Harper & Row, 1971.

Rabinow, Paul. *Reflections on Fieldwork in Morocco.* Berkeley, CA: University of California Press, 1977.

Relethford, John. *Fundamentals of Biological Anthropology.* 3d ed. Mountain View, CA: Mayfield, 1996.

Robbins, Richard H. *Global Problems and the Culture of Capitalism.* Needham Heights, MA: Allyn & Bacon, 1999.

Rosaldo, Renato. *Culture and Truth: The Remaking of Social Analysis.* Boston: Beacon Press, 1989.

Sacks, Karen. *Sisters and Wives*. Westport, CT: Greenwood Press, 1979.

Sahlins, Marshall. *Stone Age Economics*. Chicago: Aldine, 1972.

Salzmann, Zdenek. *Language, Culture and Society: An Introduction to Linguistic Anthropology*. 2d ed. Boulder, CO: Westview Press, 1998.

Savage-Rumbaugh, Sue et al. "Spontaneous Symbol Acquisition and Communicative Use by Pygmy Chimpanzees (Pan Paniscus)." *Journal of Experimental Psychology: General* 115 (1986): 211–35.

Schneider, David. *American Kinship*. Englewood Cliffs, NJ: Prentice-Hall, 1968.

———. *A Critique of the Study of Kinship*. Ann Arbor: University of Michigan Press, 1984.

Schuler, Sindey Ruth. *The Other Side of Polyandry*. Boulder, CO: Westview Press, 1987.

Schultz, Emily. *Dialogue at the Margins: Whorf, Bakhtin, and Linguistic Relativity*. Madison: University of Wisconsin, 1990.

Schwartz, Theodore, Geoffrey White, and Catherine A. Lutz, eds. *New Directions in Psychological Anthropology*. Cambridge: Cambridge University Press, 1992.

Scott, James. *Weapons of the Weak*. New Haven, CT: Yale University Press, 1987.

———. *Domination and the Arts of Resistance*. New Haven, CT: Yale University Press, 1992.

Service, Elman. *Primitive Social Organization*. New York: Random House, 1962.

———. *Origins of the State and Civilization*. New York: Norton, 1975.

Smedley, Audrey. *Race in North America*. 2d ed. Boulder, CO: Westview, 1999.

Stone, Linda. *Kinship and Gender: An Introduction*. Boulder, CO: Westview Press, 1997.

———, ed. *New Directions in Anthropological Kinship*. Lanham, MD: Rowman & Littlefield Publishers, 2001.

Strathern, Marilyn. *Reproducing the Future: Anthropology, Kinship, and the New Reproductive Technologies*. New York: Routledge, 1992.

Suggs, David, and Andrew Miracle. *Culture and Human Sexuality*. Pacific Grove, CA: Brooks/Cole, 1993.

Tambiah, Stanley. *Leveling Crowds: Nationalist Conflict and Collective Violence in South Asia*. Berkeley: University of California Press, 1997.

Van Willigen, John. *Applied Anthropology*. Rev. ed. Westport, CT: Bergin & Garvey, 1993.

Wallace, Anthony F. C. *Religion: An Anthropological View*. New York: Random House, 1966.

Weatherford, Jack. *The History of Money*. New York: Crown, 1997.

Weismantel, Mary. *Food, Gender, and Poverty in the Ecuadorian Andes*. Prospect Heights, IL: Waveland Press, 1998.

Weston, Kath. *Families We Choose: Lesbians, Gays, Kinship*. New York: Columbia University Press, 1991.

―――. "Lesbian/Gay Studies in the House of Anthropology." *Annual Review of Anthropology* 22 (1993): 339–67.

Wilk, Richard. *Economies and Cultures: Foundations of Economic Anthropology*. Boulder, CO: Westview Press, 1996.

Williams, Brackette. "A Class Act: Anthropology and the Race to Nation across Ethnic Terrain." *Annual Review of Anthropology* 18 (1989): 401–44.

Wolf, Eric. *Peasants*. Englewood Cliffs, NJ: Prentice-Hall, 1962.

―――. *Europe and the People without History*. Berkeley: University of California Press, 1982.

―――. *Envisioning Power: Ideologies of Dominance and Resistance*. Berkeley: University of California Press, 1999.

Index

Key terms are defined on boldface page numbers.